Selena,

Wonderful meeting [you?]
for the storm and [?]
it!

[signature]

# UNDRESSED

# UNDRESSED

**THE UNFILTERED STORY OF MY FAILED AMERICAN DREAM
AND HOW IT LED TO SUCCESS**

GREGORY VETTER

Homegrown Publishing | West River, MD

**Disclaimer**

I've been an athlete all my life, and if there's one thing I've learned, it's that every play has multiple POVs. The home team sees it one way, the visitors another. Then there are the officials, coaches, fans in the stands, the multitudes who will watch the clip on YouTube and race to the comments to weigh in.

But memory is a funny thing. We may all be on the field at the same time, but remember the event differently. Memories can become what we need them to be.

This is the story of what I saw and learned building my company. And this is the way I remember it.

**Note:** Apart from my family members, close associates, and public figures, names and identifiers have been changed.

© 2024 Gregory L. Vetter

All rights reserved. No part of this publication may be reproduced, stored in a retrieval sys-tem, or transmitted in any form or by any means electronic, mechanical, photocopying, re-cording or otherwise, without the prior written permission of the publisher.

Published by
Homegrown Publishing | West River, MD

        Publisher's Cataloging-in-Publication Data
        Vetter, Gregory L.

        Undressed : the unfiltered story of my failed American dream
        and how it led to success / by Gregory L. Vetter. – West River,
        MD : Homegrown Pub., 2024.

        p. ; cm.

        ISBN13: 978-0-9601277-0-2

        1. Vetter, Gregory L. 2. Success--United States--Biography.
        I. Title.

        CT121.V47 2024
        920.02--dc23

Project coordination by Jenkins Group, Inc. | www.jenkinsgroupinc.com

*Front cover design by Moe Taylor*
*Back and flap cover layout by T. Dewayne Johnson*
*Interior design by Brooke Camfiled*

Printed in the United States of America
28 27 26 25 24 • 5 4 3 2 1

# Contents

| | |
|---|---|
| **INTRODUCTION** | vii |
| **ONE** | 1 |
| **TWO** | 11 |
| **THREE** | 29 |
| **FOUR** | 51 |
| **FIVE** | 61 |
| **SIX** | 73 |
| **SEVEN** | 91 |
| **EIGHT** | 113 |
| **NINE** | 123 |
| **TEN** | 139 |
| **ELEVEN** | 155 |
| **TWELVE** | 169 |
| **THIRTEEN** | 185 |
| **FOURTEEN** | 205 |
| **FIFTEEN** | 219 |
| **SIXTEEN** | 233 |
| **EPILOGUE** | 247 |
| **ACKNOWLEDGMENTS** | 257 |
| **ABOUT THE AUTHOR** | 261 |

# Introduction

On a clear winter night, I struck a match and set fire to what was left of my company.

Not the headquarters or warehouses or production plants. Those were long since padlocked.

Instead, I stood on a patch of land on my Maryland farm, before a stack of wooden pallets and crates—all of which I'd salvaged months ago for this exact purpose: to light a bonfire and watch the last pieces of my business go up in smoke. Tessemae's All Natural would go out like a Viking, I decided, on a funeral pyre fit for a battle-scarred warrior.

My original plan was to do this when everything was officially, finally, decidedly over. Signed, done, finished. But lawyers dragged it on, as lawyers do, because they work by the hour, so longer is better and forever is best. My wife was getting tired of seeing a mountain of scrap wood piled on our property. She was right; it was getting to be an eyesore. And practically speaking, I'd said goodbye to the business over a year ago. I felt that shift in my gut that told me it was time.

I piled the pallets and crates high and invited the Tessemae's faithful to be part of the finale.

Everyone brought something to toss onto the fire. My brothers Matt and Brian brought a Tessemae's hat and a Tessemae's bottle. Moe, our creative director, threw in a Tessemae's tee shirt. Kristen, our chef, tossed one of her cooking tools into the fire—I think it was a whisk. I had one of the aprons we used to wear at the production sites. I balled it up and threw it in.

Our families were there. My wife and my four kids.

My mom and dad came, too. They just observed.

It was a little windy that night, but the fire burned straight and high. I think the flames were jumping twenty feet. I looked up as they reached for the stars in the sky. I could relate. Aiming for the stars was what I had always been about.

I knew it was time for this bonfire. I knew it was time—actually, I'd already started—to launch a new business journey. And I knew it was time to tell this story about how we created a company, grew it to be valued at over 300 million dollars, sold it out at a bankruptcy auction for 4.5 million, and the hard lessons we learned along the way.

Most people who write books do it to trumpet their success stories. Someday, that will be me. But that's not this book. This book is different. This book will tell you what can go wrong, what you can learn from those moments, and how it all shapes you as a human being, a business owner, and a warrior.

Would you like to know about that? Would you like to know what it's like to take your mother's homemade salad dressing, grow it to No. 1 in its category, pioneer a method of "clean manufacturing" that pumps out a product free of artificial gums on a mass scale, win accolades and awards and invitations to appear in a reality TV show—and then have it all go away?

Would you like to know what that roller coaster is like, what it feels like to ride it, and what you'll know when the ride ends?

Have I got a story for you.

Pull down that lap bar and hang on.

# ONE

It all started because my mom had three growing boys who refused to eat their vegetables.

My mother took her mother-protector role seriously. She was a stay-at-home mom, and my dad worked as an executive in the non-profit world.

She also taught Pilates. But her focus in our early years was on raising us, and she could be hard core. Here's an example: We played sports throughout our childhoods, starting with T-ball and soccer and moving into lacrosse in high school. My youngest brother, Matt, and I played defense, and my middle brother, Brian, was on offense. Brian wore No. 5. And during games, she was always on the sidelines, yelling, "Do something, No. 5! Do! Some! Thing!"

No Sports Dad in the league could match her drive to win.

So, it's no surprise that when we wouldn't eat our greens, she didn't let that slide. Instead, she attacked the problem and created a solution: her own homemade secret recipe salad dressing.

We loved it. We ate salads like they were ice cream sundaes.

Score one for Mom.

Team sports played a huge role in our development. We went to a rough public school in Annapolis. There was a lot of fighting and a low-level sense of hopelessness that surrounded the place. This was not yacht-club Annapolis. This was subsidized-housing Annapolis. I can walk into any business in Annapolis right now and find a janitor I went to school with. This was not a school where grades were a status factor. But athletics was a ticket to popularity. If you were a sports star, you were a success. Everyone played sports.

I remember how I discovered lacrosse. I was ten, playing baseball in a local league and wanted to be a pitcher, but of course, that position went to the coach's son. I was stashed in the outfield. And I'm standing out there one day, and there's all these ground bees swarming around me, and I'm getting stung and thinking: This sucks. I look over at the next field, and there are all these kids in helmets running around with sticks beating the shit out of each other.

I had my mom's aggressive streak and my father's curiosity, and I knew right then: that was the game for me.

My brothers followed me into the sport. It was a great outlet to be fast and aggressive, and we loved it. Lacrosse really surfaced our personalities. I wasn't the best player, but I was a grinder and would never back down from a fight. My position: defense. My brother Brian is a big shit-talker. Very flashy, very middle finger. He played offense while my mom shouted from the sidelines.

Our youngest brother Matt, we called him The Rattlesnake. He'd seem chill and not dangerous until provoked. Then, without warning, he'd strike. His position: long stick middie. Good luck to the guys who pressed his buttons.

I was always the captain of our sports teams. And as the Oldest Brother, I took on the responsibility to be the captain of our own family of boys. We were a team, we three, and I was going to blaze the trail for us.

Lacrosse was not just our sport in high school, it was our ticket to college. I played D3 lacrosse for Washington College. Brian played for Towson, which is essentially Maryland State. Matt got into Yale. He was always the most thoughtful of us brothers. He was the little kid who played with Legos and had plenty of off-field interests. But he turned Yale down and followed Brian to the Towson lacrosse team. We were close, and our team of brothers was important to all three of us.

In college, I was exposed to wealth and power for the first time. Up until that point, I thought being rich automatically made you a happier, more superior person. But I began to see a different reality. I remember consoling a friend once on his birthday. He was upset, he told me, because his birthday meant he was now "cut off from his family." When I didn't understand, he elaborated: He had a trust fund that kicked in on this birthday, and from then on, he'd need to live solely on that trust fund—a ten-million-dollar trust fund.

Befuddled, and with great anticipation of hearing about what riches would be in store for me, I called my dad. Did I have a trust fund?

My dad howled with laughter. He caught his breath long enough to say, "Son, I *trust* you'll have fun. You're on your own."

On the one hand, it was disappointing to learn there wasn't a ten-million-dollar pot of gold with my name on it in the family basement. On the other hand, my ten-million-dollar trust fund friend was miserable on his birthday. I started to realize that many of my friends at college had a burden. Their family success had been built on real estate, investment banking, law, medicine. They were expected to follow in these footsteps. They had to keep up with the Joneses in a way that I did not.

When I learned that rich people aren't necessarily special, a portal in my brain unlocked. It's easy to think that your life is predetermined by your parents or your background, but I quickly realized that was nothing more than a cop-out. I had a realization that maybe I didn't come from money, but my life was mine to make. The only expectations I had to meet were my own. And they were big: I wanted to build a company. I wanted to be like the companies I read about in

*Inc. Magazine* and *Fast Company*. I wanted to live a life of adventure that was worth living.

When college ended and the framework of sports ended, I found myself in unfamiliar territory. I played pro lacrosse for pennies, and I coached young players. But lacrosse could no longer be my whole life, as it basically had been since I was ten years old. I was in the Real World now. I needed to get a job.

At twenty-three, I had ambition spilling out of my pores and nowhere to pour it. I went for a sales gig because I wanted to determine my commission and salary. I took a job selling insurance. There was nothing glamorous about the company's office above a bodega overlooking a cemetery, but all I needed was a dial tone. I cold-called my dick off. Phones slammed before I could say hello. Receptionists told me to fuck off. With each rejection, something in me grew stronger. Resolve? Will? Masochism? I wasn't sure at the time. Sales makes you confront your innate fear of rejection. You either get over it and become successful or look for another career path. The competitive element of sales hooked me right away. It was the successor to lacrosse. There was a spectrum of relativity for winning. You could always be better, attain more.

I was good at it. I brought in three of the top five clients for the company and was sure this would help me to move up. So, I asked for a sit down with my boss, and he suggested lunch at this local Mexican café known for its margaritas. One margarita was amazing. Two, you're drunk. Three, you are fucked.

We sat down to have a chat about my future.

"I have brought in three of the top five clients for your company, I have built out your sales team from nothing, and I want to be a partn . . ."

My boss immediately cut me off and said, "NO!"

"Why not?" I asked.

"You make a lot of money, and I'm not letting you get a piece of my entire company. You don't need it."

Stunned, I played it off like he was right and understood his position. I tried to make my reaction sound like I didn't care that he had just smashed my ambitions, hopes, and dreams. But in that moment, sitting outside some piece of shit café on a dilapidated picnic table one moonshine margarita deep, I made the decision to start something. My boss' ignorant response lit a fire in my soul, and I was going to do something about it. He had given me the greatest gift anyone could have received in a dead-end job, a clear answer about what the future holds. Most people stay where they are because of "analysis paralysis." Is the grass really greener on the other side? Is what I am leaving behind really that bad? I didn't need to worry about those questions any longer because I knew the answer. But now I needed to figure out what I was going to do.

## My Quest Begins

The next day at lunch, instead of eating at my cubicle, I went home and started my new routine. I called it: Finding an epiphany. I would turn the lights off in my bedroom, put a pillow on the ground, and do a headstand against the wall with my eyes closed, asking myself, "What am I going to do with the rest of my life?"

My assumption was that all that blood being in my brain would make my brain work at a higher frequency, and then I would have an epiphany. Days went by, then weeks, then months, and the routine didn't change. I would leave my cubicle and drive home. I would walk up to my bedroom, put a pillow on the ground, and stand on my head until I felt like I was going to pass out.

While standing on my head, I would think about what I wanted to do with my life and hope to have an epiphany. If any ideas popped into my mind, I would get out of my headstand and write them down.

Once I reached the point of pain, I would walk downstairs and make myself a big salad—with my mom's own dressing and some protein on top.

One day in February, after my headstand routine, I went into my kitchen to make my lunch and my salad dressing was missing. The dressing that was missing was my mom's famous Lemon Garlic dressing, which she had made for me and my brothers when we were kids so we would eat our veggies. Twenty years later, she was still making it once a month in two-liter bottles for all of us to consume. Some moms bake cookies. Mine slings salad dressing.

The bottle was too big for the refrigerator, so I would keep mine on the counter for easy access.

But on this fateful day, it was nowhere to be seen.

My kitchen was not big, so my initial thought was that I was either blind or losing my mind. Continuing to be dazed and confused, I opened all the cabinets, opened the refrigerator, and scoured every inch of the kitchen. In frustration, I called my wife, Genevieve.

"Did you move the salad dressing or take it with you to work?"

"The what?" she asked.

"The salad dressing. The big bottle of my mom's salad dressing. Have you seen it? Did you move it somewhere?"

She could hear the frustration in my voice and laughed a little. "Ha, maybe one of our neighbors came in and took it."

I wasn't amused by her joke. "Someone came and took the dressing? What the hell are you talking about?"

She laughed some more. "I don't know, Greg. Just call around. I don't have any other suggestions for you."

So, I started calling our neighbors. I narrowed the call list down to those who ate salads.

"Hey, man, have you seen my salad dressing?"

The common response was laughter and then, "No, man. I did not take your salad dressing."

I finally called a friend. Smitty was the least likely culprit to be eating a salad. We played lacrosse together, and he wasn't the salad type. He hustled lacrosse gear, did lacrosse lessons, and sold smokes on the side. He loved fast food and wasn't your typical salad eater. But I was out of reasonable suspects.

"Smitty, have you seen my salad dressing?" He sounded like he was eating right at the moment and replied, "Yuuuppppp, woke up this morning jonesing for it." So, he hopped on his scooter, made his way to my house, used the key code (and I could not remember why I'd given it to him) and now, he was in salad heaven.

"I'm crushing a salad." *Chomp chomp chomp. Gulp.* "Do you want me to bring it back?"

I tried to wrap my head around the fact that Smitty had committed burglary to steal my mom's homemade salad dressing. "Uh, yeah!" I replied. So, through his chewing, Smitty promised to scooter right over and return it. "Be right there, bud."

I hung up and stood there in shock, asking myself over and over again: What kind of man steals another man's salad dressing?

Then, a life-altering question emerged: What kind of salad dressing is worth stealing?

I started to answer my own question. It is good. No one has ever been able to replicate it. Everyone that has ever tried it loves it. Every lacrosse tailgate my mom ever brought it to, it was the talk of the team. And this was with a bunch of meatheads who reveled in being human garbage disposals.

Salads will always need dressing.

Bottled salad dressing sucks.

Why isn't there a fresh salad dressing this good you can buy?

There has to be.

But what if there isn't?

That moment, I was not in a headstand, but apparently, yelling at Smitty had pushed enough blood to my brain to get the idea of ideas.

The epiphany: I am going to start a salad dressing company! But wait, great-tasting salad dressing has to exist, right? I can't have just had a completely original idea, right?

After repeating that line of questioning in my mind over and over again, I decided to pressure test the idea with Genevieve and called her back.

"Smitty stole the salad dressing."

She laughed. "Typical Smitty."

Then I said, "I'm going to quit my job and start a salad dressing company."

I paused and waited for her reaction. She paused, too. I could almost hear the wheels turning in her brain as she pondered the idea on the other end of the telephone connection.

And then she said it. "That's the best idea I have ever heard. This is going to work. I just have a feeling."

"Really?! I did not expect you to have that response."

Genevieve laughed. "This is going to work, Greg."

## Field Guide: Lessons Learned

*Welcome to the Field Guide. A section just like this one will appear at the end of every chapter. It will summarize my takeaways and lessons learned. I will keep them short and sweet so you can reference them often as your own business journey unfolds.*

### What You Need to Know

Be careful what you wish for, and don't judge the package your wish arrives in.

### How to Do It

We dream big dreams and when they are delivered on a silver platter, we don't recognize them because they're not as we imagined them arriving. Write your dreams down and then put in place a plan to achieve them down to the smallest detail. When you figure out how complicated and intricate the plan will need to be to achieve the dream, your brain will start to look for shortcuts on how to accomplish the dream faster.

### What You Need to Know
Omens or signs come when you are open to receiving them and still enough to hear them.

### How to Do It
In this world of chaos, find quiet and think. The answers you are searching for are waiting for your quiet mind. Every morning, before your day and the chaos begins, set aside fifteen minutes to one hour and think. Set the time aside to let your brain wonder, but keep a pad of paper near you in case there is an epiphany.

### What You Need to Know
Be bold enough to say the idea out loud and pressure test it with the people you care about.

### How to Do It
Write down the idea first. Then do some surface-level research. It can be as simple as Googling the idea to see what pops up. If there are fifty businesses already doing the idea you have, ask yourself how yours would be different. Map out how it would be different and put some preliminary research into it. Then nonchalantly bring up your idea to people who will give you some quick, honest feedback.

The old saying, "When one door closes, another one opens" is true. Be bold enough to say the idea out loud and pressure test it with the people you care about. Saying it out loud and waiting for the reaction will be the easiest part of your idea's journey. You never know unless you try. The feeling in your gut is the universe trying to tell you something.

# TWO

I hung up the phone and moved on to my next pressure test: my mom.

Still standing in my kitchen, waiting for Smitty the Thief to scooter over and return my dressing, I called her. "Mom, I'm going to take your dressing recipe and start a salad dressing company."

I paused and waited for her reaction. It didn't take long.

"That's the worst idea I have ever heard. That's never going to work."

My mom doesn't pull punches. But I am just as direct. Even in my very unfiltered family, I'm known as the cold, hard truth-teller. I replied, "Well, I *am* starting the company with or without you and I *am* going to need the recipe because I *am* getting it into grocery stores." She laughed, and I hung up.

I began my quest using the only business skill I knew: cold calling. I Googled the Annapolis location of a natural foods chain and called their main number.

"Hi, can I speak with someone about my world-famous salad dressing?"

"Yes, hold, please."

Someone picked up, and I went for it. "Hi, I live in Annapolis and have a world-famous salad dressing, and I would like for your store to carry it."

The person on the other end of this call must have taken communication lessons from my mother. "Not interested. Thanks." And then hung up.

But that hang up did not feel right. It was not an informed business decision. The woman on the phone was too quick and didn't ask any questions. I wasn't convinced that was a real, final "No."

I decided I needed to know more about my target. I reached out to a family friend who worked for the natural foods chain in their regional office. She explained to me that an individual store could bring in a product, just to that one location, at their discretion. The trick was to speak to the right person. And, no, she didn't know who that was at the Annapolis store.

So, I committed myself to finding that person. I called the Annapolis natural foods store twice a day for two weeks. My assumption was that there was a shift change at some point in the morning, so I called first thing when they opened and then again around four p.m. Everyone I spoke to said no.

Then one Friday morning, I hit the bullseye. Instead of no, I advanced. "You need to speak to James. Let me get him for you." When James picked up, I gave him my pitch, and he said, "Yeah, bring it down today around noon, and I'll look at it."

AHHHHHHHHHHHH! VICTORY!

I called my mom. "I need you to make the greatest batch of salad dressing you have ever made, NOW!"

"Why Greg? What is going on?"

"I have a meeting with the natural foods chain today at noon!"

I drove to my parent's house. My mom wouldn't shut up: *You're not a company! You don't have a bottle! How are you going to do this?*

"Mom, just make the dressing, and I'll take care of the rest."

She did. We put it in a red-lid Tupperware container over crunchy romaine lettuce, and I hauled ass over to the natural foods store, marched in, and asked for James.

James was a presence. He was black, about fifty, missing some teeth on the right side of his mouth. He looked like a former boxer you did not want to fuck with. His demeanor fit that profile. "Where is it?" he demanded, not smiling.

I held up my Tupperware container. He looked at me, puzzled. "Well, it's lunchtime. I know you are busy, so I brought you a salad."

James's face went from puzzled to concerned, like maybe I was on drugs and trying to sell him stolen DVDs. He stared at me for a while, and I just smiled and nodded my head "yes" to encourage him to try it.

He opened the Tupperware container, picked out a piece of wet romaine lettuce with his hands, and licked the dressing off. He didn't even eat the lettuce. But as the dressing hit his taste buds, his eyes lit up, and he looked at me. "You got something real special here. You need to call the regional office."

I pushed my moment. "Can you call the regional office for me, and I'll show up to the meeting?" He laughed and said he would.

The next day, thanks to James's introduction, I had a call with Michael at the natural foods chain's mid-Atlantic offices. Michael was the director of produce for the region and was busy opening the new Annapolis store a couple of miles away from the one where I met James. Michael got right to the point. "James told me it's good. Bring it to me today at ten a.m." I drove down with my sample. Michael was Boston-born, and the minute I walked into the store, he said, "You look like Tom Brady! Where's this world-famous dressing?"

I handed him the Tupperware container of romaine lettuce and watched for his reaction. He took a piece of wet lettuce out of the container, ate the lettuce, and immediately said, "We want to have you for the grand opening of this Annapolis store in May. I'll send you the paperwork. If you get it done, we'll let you sample your product for the grand opening week. But that's all I am committing to."

I smiled, shook his hand, thanked him for the time, and sprinted to the car. I called Genevieve and told her the news. "THIS IS GOING TO WORK!" Genevieve started laughing and then gave me an "atta boy" over the phone and said, "Told ya." I called my mom and let her know we were going to be in the Annapolis store for the grand opening. She was shocked. As I drove home to look at the paperwork, my face wouldn't stop smiling. I had a taste of the American Dream, and I was going to do anything to finish the meal.

I sprinted into the house and opened up the email that had all the paperwork from Michael. My happiness turned to dismay as I began reading the requirements. There were 200 pages of actual food manufacturing forms that were so foreign I could have been reading the wrong documents for all I knew. The reality of what I had just set in motion sank in, and I realized, *Oh fuck, now I need to be a real food manufacturer.*

## Food Manufacturing for Dummies

When I read the first page of the documents from the natural foods chain, I couldn't understand half the shit they were asking. I had to Google half the words on the page to figure out what the word even meant, and then once I figured out what the words meant, I had to Google the answer to the question. For example, there was a section on the forms that said: "Give us your HACCP plan."

What in the fuck is a HACCP plan?

I Googled "What is a HACCP plan," and Google supplied "Hazard analysis and critical control points is a systematic preventive approach to food safety from biological, chemical, and physical hazards in production processes that can cause the finished product to be unsafe and designs measures to reduce these risks to a safe level."

*Say what?!* I didn't have that, I didn't even know what the hell they were talking about.

I thought for a moment and then Googled "HACCP plan for salad dressing," and an HACCP for salad dressing popped up. I downloaded it, printed it, and put it in my file of completed documents. This Googling process went on until I was asked a simple but vital question: Name of Company. I still didn't have the most critical piece of the journey I was trying to embark on: our brand and name.

It's kind of funny to think about it now. We got the opportunity with the natural foods chain before we even had a name. I started brainstorming and writing potential brand names down. And everything I was writing down was complete trash.

"3 Brothers Salad Dressing"

"Greg's Own"

"Lemon Zingers"

I knew they sucked, but I pressure tested the names to see what Genevieve thought of them, and her face said it all: It looked like she had just smelled a horrible fart.

I went back to the drawing board and started to think about what brand name would work. What type of company could people get behind? Something real, something that told a story, something that was timeless, and then I wrote down Tessemae's Organic. My mom's email address used Tessemae in it and Tessemae's sounded like a real company. The more I thought about it, the more I liked it. I could make the entire brand about a mom who couldn't get her boys to eat their vegetables and came up with this amazing dressing to win over their taste buds. And now, not only do they eat their veggies, but they are bringing that same dressing to the world. The entire brand unfolded before my eyes as I stared at the name written on the blank piece of copy paper. And the best part was, it was actually true.

I went on to GoDaddy.com to see if Tessemaes.com was available, and it was. I sketched out a logo with the name above it and showed it to Genevieve. She smiled from ear to ear. "It's really good, Greg." I smiled because I believed her and knew she was right.

Now we were official. We set up the company on LegalZoom, and *boom* Tessemae's LLC was a thing. I called a guy I played lacrosse with who was a graphic designer to design the website and label for the dressing, and he did it for $2,000. Now we were making some moves. We had a name, a website, a chance to go into the natural foods chain, and now I just needed to figure out how to be a food manufacturer. I was now entering the real part of the paperwork that I couldn't Google my way through: kitchen location, packaging design, food science approvals, etc. The most difficult part to bring to life in such a short time was securing the location that would allow us to get our food manufacturing license. I had no idea where to start and just started Googling "certified kitchens to rent." If anything within an hour's drive popped up, I would call. "Hi, I literally know nothing about what I'm talking about and have a chance to get into a natural foods chain, will you please help me get this done?"

Every person was receptive to my request, but finding a "move-in ready" place that I could afford on such a short turnaround was starting to feel impossible. I started asking people to point me in the right direction. Some people said churches. Some said restaurants. Some said just co-pack it. (Co-pack is an industry term for hiring out the physical manufacturing of a food product.) I didn't know which way was up.

But that week, serendipity was on my side. I had a meeting with Robert, who owned a leasing firm, to sell him insurance for his employees (I did still have a sales job at this juncture.) Robert also happened to be part owner of The Rolling Bones, a local rib restaurant. That meant nothing to me at the time, but as I was pitching him on being his benefits broker, he cut me off and said he was too busy to keep the meeting going and needed to run. "Go where?" I asked.

The funny thing about Robert is that he loves to bitch. You name it, he will bitch about it. He took my question as an opening to do just that. "My general manager quit at the restaurant, I need to get my knee checked out from this marathon I just ran, I have to find a new salad dressing for the restaurant because the current one sucks—"

I stopped him right there and told him I had a salad dressing he should use. He laughed. "Oh yeah, what is it?" he asked sarcastically. I told him I just launched a salad dressing company and he should try it. He looked skeptical until I told him about the grand opening.

Robert said he would try it. I drove straight home, got the salad dressing, and brought it back to him. He called me the next day. "It is the best salad dressing I've ever had. I actually can't believe it. Initially, it's mild and delicious, and then the lemon comes in at the end like a soft summer breeze."

Soft summer breeze? I started laughing. "You should be our spokesperson!" He said he would love to use it at The Rolling Bones, so I told him we could start shipping to him as soon as we launched at the natural foods chain. I didn't mention the fact that we didn't have a kitchen—because I had a bit of a secret plan.

## Launch of the Secret Plan

I waited about a week before I called him back and asked to use The Rolling Bones as our certified kitchen space. He said no. He didn't want the health department doing unnecessary audits at his restaurant for a company that wasn't his.

I continued my search with no success. I was running out of time. Then came the moment of truth: I had to submit the paperwork for the manufacturing license, or we wouldn't make the deadline for the grand opening. I called Robert one more time, begging to use The Rolling Bones, and his response was the same as before. "No. Not going to happen. I'm going on vacation for two weeks, I'll try and help you when I get back, but you cannot use The Rolling Bones."

Fuck!

I had nothing else even close to a possible option, and I couldn't wait for two weeks for him to get back to help me.

So, I put his address down on the forms anyway.

I bet on myself being able to convince him to say yes. After I filed the license application, the health department called, and I scheduled the walk-through for a week after Robert got back from vacation to give him plenty of time to say no multiple more times before saying yes.

At the same time, I needed to get the packaging approved by the state health department. I called the office, and they said it would take three to six months to get packaging approved for a product like mine since it was a new company. I dialed up the intensity. "Listen, ma'am, my life is on the line here. I have a shot to get into a natural foods chain and this is the only thing standing in my way. I'll literally do anything for you to fast-track this approval."

There was a pause, and she replied, "I take my lunch in thirty minutes. Be in the lobby, and I'll take a look."

Great! Except her offices were forty-five minutes away.

I jumped out of my cubicle and ran to my car. I drove as fast as my car would go, breaking every law you could break while driving a vehicle. Thirty minutes later, I was standing in the lobby holding a bottle of salad dressing in the air like the Statue of Liberty.

She got off the elevator and walked up to me. "I assume you're Greg?" Looking over my bottle and paperwork, she discovered a problem: We didn't have a seal mechanism on the bottle. She explained we needed a sealing machine of some sort, which aren't very cheap or easy to use. I went with the only idea that popped into my head: Booze. "Maker's Mark uses wax!" I blurted out. "That doesn't look like a sealing machine seal to me."

She laughed and agreed that wax provides the same tamper-proof safety seal needed as a sealing machine, and we could use wax if we wanted. "Well then, we use wax," I said with confidence.

With a smirk, she said the packaging was approved—pending me sending her a picture of the bottle sealed with wax. I thanked her a million times and told her she just earned herself free salad dressing for life. One major item accomplished, one more to go. And this was the big one: the certified kitchen.

Robert got back from vacation, and I drove to see him, with my intensity in full gear. "Listen, man, I know you don't care about my stupid salad dressing company, but I'll give you anything to let me use your restaurant when you guys are closed. I'll give you salad dressing for life! Anything!"

He moaned and groaned, and then said, "I don't want you stealing stuff at night."

I laughed out loud. "Stealing stuff?! What? Uncooked meat and fountain sodas?!"

He also started to laugh. "Alright, man, but if you make this a hassle for any of my people, you are done."

I gave him a big hug. "You are The Man. The state inspectors will be here next Wednesday for the walk-through."

Robert's eyes nearly shot out of his head. "Next Wednesday?! Did you already set it up here?!"

I explained I had to file the application with an address to make the deadline, and I knew he would do the right thing. He chuckled and said if the health department "dinged" The Rolling Bones for my bullshit, he was going to be pissed. I promised him he had nothing to worry about.

The day of the inspection had arrived, and I met the inspector at the restaurant. He walked through my little area with a measuring tape, checked distances from the floor, temps in the refrigerator, etc. We walked out to the parking lot, and he explained to me he would let me know in three weeks. Which was way too long. "Sir, I have a lot going on right now with trying to pull off this miracle. Can you just let me know now how it went?"

He explained that a rack in the refrigerator was an inch too close to the ground and a hinge on the refrigerator door was slightly loose, so he wasn't going to give me the license and was going to write a citation to The Rolling Bones! I screamed, "NO! You cannot do that. I'll go in there right now and fix whatever you need. This is the only place that would let me use their space for this manufacturing license, and if you write them up, I AM FUCKED. Please, for the love of everything holy, don't do that." He looked a little puzzled and paused. I sat there with both my hands together in prayer position, giving puppy dog eyes until he spoke. "If you go fix those two things right now, I will give you the license and ignore them."

I gave the guy a huge hug and ran back inside to fix the violations. I ran back outside with pictures on my phone of the improvements, and the guy hesitantly wrote up my passing grade. He handed me a piece of paper. "I hope you make this into something special." I hugged him again and told him, "You are a part of the story now. It has to work!"

I called Robert to let him know the walk-through was very uneventful, and he had nothing to worry about, just like I predicted. As a veteran restaurant man, Robert was surprised by my report.

"There was literally nothing? They always find something."

"Nope, it was all good. Very easy."

Robert couldn't believe it and told me I was lucky. I said maybe I am.

The manufacturing license came, and I sent over all the final paperwork to the natural foods chain. Tessemae's Organic was about to go live! The website looked great. I made business cards. I ordered embroidered aprons to wear for the demo. All the dressing was made. We had found cheap candles at the local big box crafts chain to melt down and use for the dipping wax so the bottles looked official. I printed the labels and had the printer custom cut them to fit perfectly on the bottle. We were ready. Four cases of salad dressing—forty-eight bottles of liquid gold, ready to change the salad dressing world.

The day before the grand opening, I received a call from Michael asking for our organic certification of the facility.

"Umm, we don't have one. We use The Rolling Bones kitchen. All the ingredients are organic in the product. I can send over the ingredients list."

Michael explained that without the organic facility certification, the product couldn't be called organic, and we couldn't use organic in the name. News to me. But I acted like it was no big deal. "Really? OK . . . not a problem . . . it will be fixed by tomorrow"

I hung up the phone. Holy fuck. This thing is going down tomorrow. And everything is wrong.

I quickly changed the name to Tessemae's All Natural from Tessemae's Organic. To do that, I needed my graphic designer/website guy to change the logo and then fix the label and the website. I called him four times. He finally sent me a text—a picture of him on a tube floating down a lazy river drinking beer. He was on vacation, and I was about to see my brand-new company dead and floating away right next to him before it could debut.

I texted back, "I will pay you anything you need to get off that tube. I need an emergency change to everything." After a phone call to explain the situation, he agreed to make the emergency changes. It took him about an hour, and he charged me $2,000 for the inconvenience of interrupting his tube time.

While he got back to his beers and lazy river, I ran to the copy store and printed new labels. While they were custom cutting the new labels to my bottle size, I called the embroidery place and had them do a rush order for new aprons. With the labels in hand and the aprons freshly embroidered, I went back to my house and relabeled forty-eight bottles of dressing. It was a later night than I had expected, and honestly, it was a small taste of what the future was going to hold. I went to bed with butterflies in my stomach like a kid on Christmas Eve. Tomorrow was going to be a very interesting morning in regard to my grandiose ideas of entrepreneurial excellence.

## Game Day

I arrived at the natural foods store at 7:30 a.m. to make sure we were in the best place for a demo and to scope out the scene. Every C-suite and regional executive was walking the aisles of the Annapolis store. I found Michael and asked him where I should set up. He tried to put me in the back by the dressing, but I convinced him to let me set up by the berries right when you walked in the front doors. "People are going to want a sample right when they walk in," I told him. He was too busy with getting the store set up to argue with me.

As the clock ticked down to game time, a crowd formed outside of the doors. I looked at my watch and it was only 8:30 a.m. By 9:45 a.m., it looked like a bunch of teenagers waiting to see The Beatles come out of their hotel. I built as many little samples as I could possibly fit on the demo table, knowing that they were going to go fast.

The grand opening was set for ten a.m., Tuesday, May 5, 2009, and we partnered with a local lettuce company for the demo, so we didn't have to buy lettuce. I set up the table and positioned Tessemae's as the main focus, with a side pyramid stack of the local lettuce. As I was preparing the samples, the woman from the lettuce company kept telling me, "You're putting too much dressing on the lettuce. People really want to be able to enjoy the flavor of the lettuce!" I did not say, "Shut the fuck up. No one cares about lettuce." But the glare I gave her must have said it all because she didn't press the issue.

As ten a.m. approached, I started praying. I prayed this salad dressing idea would work. I prayed that no one from my day job would walk through those doors. And I prayed the day would go smoothly.

The doors opened, and people started rushing into the store. We were the first thing people saw, so everyone stopped at our table to try our product. I started handing out samples and trying to tell people my story. "Would you like a sample? This is my salad dressing company. It's my mom's recipe, and you have to try it."

I couldn't hand out samples fast enough, and by 10:30 a.m., four cases of twelve bottles had been sold. I went to Michael to let him know.

"I'm out of salad dressing," I said.

"There is more in the back," he replied.

"No, there isn't. I sold the four cases."

He was fucking shocked. "You sold forty-eight bottles of salad dressing in thirty minutes?! Go get more!"

I looked at him, confused. "I have to go make more! You said that's all you needed for the month!" He told me to go make six more cases for the following day because it must have been a fluke. I called Genevieve to let her know the good news. "G, I sold it all in thirty minutes. Everyone loved it." She was at work, sitting in her cubicle, so whispered back. "That's amazing. I knew this was going to work. Gotta go."

I then called my mom to make more product. "Mom, we sold out the dressing! I need you to make more. Right now!"

She quietly replied, "I'm teaching Pilates, Greg. I can't right now."

Stunned, I snapped back, "Fuck Pilates, we just sold out of the dressing. We need to go make fucking dressing!"

That didn't work on her. She whispered a quiet "No." Then she hung up.

It was now 10:35 a.m., and I had to wait until 10:30 p.m. for The Rolling Bones to close, so I could get into that kitchen and make six more cases by myself.

I arrived the next day for the demo and set up in the same place. I wore the same outfit, partnered with the same lettuce company, and nearly the same thing happened—sold all the bottles in forty-five minutes.

I went to Michael. "Hey, man, we're out of the dressing."

Michael, once again gobsmacked, said, "What the fuck are you putting in this shit? Go get more!" This time he said to make twelve cases. No way we would sell twelve more cases now that the initial hype of the grand opening was dying down.

This time, I didn't bother my mom at Pilates. I just drove home to see what else I needed to buy to make twelve cases of dressing. I was thinking I'd only need to buy ingredients, but then I realized I had another item on my shopping list—one that would be much harder to get: I was out of bottles. I had only purchased ten cases of these fancy 8.5-oz rectangular bottles with corks, thinking that was enough inventory for two months—not two days!

I started calling bottle suppliers around town, and no one carried 8.5-oz rectangular bottles with a cork. I finally called a local bottle distributor located in seen-better-days Baltimore, and a woman named Cathy picked up. "How can I help ya, sweetie?"

"Hi, Cathy. I need your help. I have a salad dressing company, and we just sold ten cases of dressing in two days, and I need an 8.5-oz rectangular bottle with a cork to keep this train moving."

She started laughing. She had a devoted smoker's vocal fry. "We ain't got that darlin', but I got a 10-oz beer bottle with a screw top. That's close to 8.5 oz. No one will know the difference."

I tried to process this substation idea. "Cathy, my current bottle is rectangular with a cork, and this is a round bottle with a screw top?"

"Yup. That's what we got, hon."

I looked at my watch. "Fuck it. I'll be there in thirty minutes."

I bought twenty cases of bottles and thanked Cathy. I called my graphic designer and had him change the label size for a 10-oz beer bottle, and then I went to the printer to pick up the new labels. This time, he only charged me his normal hourly rate for the work instead of the lazy river beer tax I paid to change the name. I rolled into The Rolling Bones at 10:30 p.m. with my brothers, made the dressing, and showed up the next day with round bottles instead of rectangular ones.

Cathy was right. No one knew the difference. Go figure. The sales results were the same. We were averaging 1.5 bottles sold per minute during my demos. No one could believe what was happening. Michael literally came to stand by my demo station to see if people were actually buying that much salad dressing or if I was just guzzling it myself. And they were. He congratulated me, still with that look of shock and awe.

At the end of the week, the new Annapolis store issued a report on the Top 10 products in every category for the grand opening week, and Tessemae's was one of the top-selling products in the produce category. The list went: bananas, lettuce, carrots . . . Tessemae's. It was fucking bananas (pun intended). We set a national sales record and sold fifty-five cases in five days of one flavor in one store. That's 660 bottles of salad dressing. We were the talk of the grand opening—those crazy brothers and their mom's salad dressing that sells like hotcakes.

By the last day, everyone was walking up to me to introduce themselves and try a sample. Every produce buyer and regional executive gave me their card and told me to call them. I started to think that this dressing idea could work on a national scale. I always filter my ideas by putting them to one immortal question: It's either *fuck yes* or *fuck no*. This salad dressing was an overwhelming *fuck yes*.

After I decompressed and reflected on the week, I decided to pressure test the actual growth prospects of getting into new stores. I called a couple of the natural foods chain's stores, which were within a quick drive, to see if they wanted to carry the product as well.

Every person I called immediately answered yes. "I heard about your stuff at the grand opening. That's crazy! How much did you end up selling?" I would tell them, "We sold 660 bottles in five days of one flavor." Every single person shouted back some version of: "I don't sell that much dressing in a year! Of course, I want you in my store!"

Getting a "yes" had never been so easy in anything I've ever done. What could this turn into?

---

## Field Guide: Lessons Learned

### What You Need to Know
You only live once. Take a risk, trust your gut, and live a life you are proud of.

### How to Do It
I read a quote once about waking up early, "Only when the rest of the world is silent can you hear its deeper vibration." When you are thinking about taking a great risk and it goes against the social norms of your close friends and family, find quiet and listen for the answer. I did this by journaling first thing in the morning, taking walks in nature, and working out without music. During those moments, I would ask myself the question I wanted an answer to, over and over. And then I would wait and listen for the answer. Your brain will try to fight an answer it doesn't like, so keep asking the question and keep listening to the answer. Even if the answer is not what you want to hear, at least you have it.

### What You Need to Know
Trust your "basic ass knowledge."

### How to Do It
I didn't know what the brand was going to be that first day in my kitchen. But there were things I did know. I knew that bottled salad dressing:

- Tasted like shit
- Wasn't cool

Don't overthink a customer's reaction to the product. Too many people overthink a category or "white space" and don't realize the everyday American consumer doesn't know what you are talking about and doesn't care. The consumer wants something that makes them happy and makes their lives easier. It's as simple as that. Bringing my "basic ass knowledge" to the table gave me the courage to disagree with the "experts" and prove my idea right.

### What You Need to Know
Prove yourself wrong. Just because it's your idea doesn't mean it's a good idea.

### How to Do It
Imagine you hire yourself as a brand and product consultant to poke holes in every aspect of the idea you have. Make yourself a "hater" for the day and look at your idea as someone who is trying to destroy it. What are the results of this process? I was convinced that clean salad dressing that tasted good had to exist. And so, I went out into the marketplace to find it. It didn't exist. I kept searching, I kept buying and trying products, but nothing was there. I was trying to prove myself wrong. It turned out, we had stumbled onto something big.

### What You Need to Know
Be a story someone wants to tell.

### How to Do It

Imagine your consumer picking up the product for the first time and ask yourself, Why do they care? What is going to get them to go home and tell their friends about it? What will make it special? Is making it special even possible? What would it take to make my story "sticky" enough to remember and then pass on? Answer all those questions and then design the brand around that.

# THREE

After making the calls to a couple of the natural foods chain's stores within driving distance, I started to think this moment might be bigger than I'd thought. Had I stumbled on a sleepy, dead category desperate for a youthful brand?

I decided to expand into four more stores: Two in Baltimore, one in Bethesda, and one in Kentlands. This would give me a good pulse on how the Maryland, DC, and Northern Virginia stores operated and what their consumers were like. At the time, the natural foods chain loved the "local brand" angle and it was a major part of their marketing campaign. But I wanted to see just how far my local brand could reach and still be impactful.

All of the initial calls to get into the local stores drew a quick "Yes!" They just wanted me to do demos as I had in the Annapolis store. Sounded good enough to me. I set up demos in each of the stores, and the results were nearly the same. Each store was a little different because of size and demographics but the "try-to-buy ratio" was spot on. If someone tried the dressing and heard the story of "three brothers and a mother living happy and healthy," they were buying it.

The only real issue I needed to solve was recreating "me," so I could be in *all* the stores at once.

## Manufacturing More Brothers

Three of me was easy because of my brothers. They tell the story just like I do, and we sell just as much. But three brothers can only do so many demos. Could we find people similar to us and have them say they were cousins? Part of the family? A brother? Would the sales be the same?

When we hooked a new store in Baltimore that was only twenty minutes from Matt's college, we tested this idea: We deployed Matt and his lacrosse buddies to do demos on Friday nights or midday Saturdays. We selected Matt's most handsome friends, the ones with outgoing personalities, and tested the waters.

They killed it.

These dudes had so much fun they asked to do it again, but on one condition: We make them business cards with their cell phone numbers on the cards so they could pick up women. Seemed like a small price to pay for one hundred bottles sold in four hours, so we agreed and officially launched our Non-Brother Demo Force. If this demo plan worked, we could scale infinitely because there were young college men in every town with a natural foods chain location. Why didn't we use young college women? Because our target market was the Millennial Mom. And the Millennial Moms loved hearing a wonderful story about a family's salad-dressing dreams from a handsome college boy athlete with entrepreneurial aspirations.

The expanded demo plan was insanely successful. The real issue then became making dressing consistently and delivering it all over the area at a moment's notice. We needed a schedule and a production plan that aligned with the stores' sales volume. Our problem was that we worked directly—and independently—with each store. We had to call each produce department on the phone and have one of the produce workers walk into the back refrigerator and count the number of cases they had. If that produce worker decided to be lazy and wrong, then we were lazy and wrong. This additional layer of chaos, combined with the making and delivering of salad dressing to four stores while working three other jobs, started to wear me down. I wanted the salad dressing business to work, but I was simultaneously selling insurance, playing professional lacrosse, and coaching an elite youth lacrosse team. Something had to give.

I found inspiration in a habit I had started in my senior year in college.

That year, I began a project of self-education and inspiration. I began interviewing CEOs and successful people to figure out how they created their success. What decisions did they make to get them to where they were? Every answer was different, and because of that, I kept finding new people to meet with and pick their brains.

As I was trying to figure out what this salad dressing business had in store for me (or didn't), I had scheduled a breakfast with John, the founder of a regional construction firm. We met at a breakfast spot in Bowie, Maryland, at seven a.m. I asked him my established set of questions, and then he gave me a quick version of his life story and how he became so successful. Then he asked me what I was up to. I told him about insurance, and lacrosse . . . no big reaction from him. And then I told him about the little salad dressing company I had started.

He perked up and wanted to hear more. By the end of our breakfast, he looked into the distance and said, "If I could do it all over again, I would do something like you are doing. I build stuff and develop stuff, but no one really cares what it is, plus my kids certainly don't think it's cool. But if I had done what you did, and I had a product to show my family, that would be cool."

I was stunned. After thanking him for his time and paying for breakfast, I walked out to my car and just sat there. John thinks the salad dressing business is the winner? That's what he would have done? I realized the "something's gotta give" wasn't going to be quitting salad dressing, it was going to be getting rid of everything else and focusing on the salad dressing.

I called Genevieve and told her about the breakfast, and told her she had to quit her job. She laughed and said we would talk about it. I called Brian and told him the same thing. He also laughed and said we would talk about it.

They both worked for the same telecom recruiting company, Genevieve as a manager, and Brian, brand new in sales. I called a meeting that night in my townhouse with both of them so we could discuss the future. And here's how I pitched it: my job did not require me to be seated where my boss could see me—I could do my job anywhere, anytime. But Genevieve and Brian both had classic office jobs that required them to be in the office every day. I said: You two quit your jobs. I'll keep mine and do it in and around my salad dressing commitments.

Brian agreed to quit his job on Monday—and he did it. We decided Genevieve wouldn't quit right away, but agreed to focus all her downtime on purchasing, planning, and running operations for the salad dressing. I would quit my job as soon as we grew the business to a point where we could pay a salary. At this stage, I was funding it with credit cards and my own cash. I took that process and revved it into high gear. I took out twenty credit cards and liquidated my 401k, which gave us enough cash to fuel some growth. Brian became our first official paid employee at 500 dollars biweekly. Genevieve liquidated her 401k and started taking her lunch breaks in her car to make calls to buy raw materials for us to make dressing. I created an Excel model: We needed to grow from four stores to eighteen stores to hit our first goal. Shit was officially on the line, and there was no fucking around.

## Morning Coffee

Every morning Brian and I would meet at Café Pronto in Annapolis after the gym at around seven a.m. and go through the day's goals and how we were tracking for the week's goals. We knew exactly how much dressing we had to make and sell to be the #1 dressing in the Mid-Atlantic region of the natural foods chain. But we had a production problem. Making dressing by hand for one store is doable. It's not efficient or easy, but it's doable. Making dressing for four stores, while at the same time doing demos in those stores, is actually pretty hard. Now that Brian was full time, we could see and solve problems and inefficiencies that we had ignored before because I was only making dressing once a week. We could see that we were maxing out the handmade production capacity at The Rolling Bones now that we were delivering and demoing in stores on a consistent basis. We had bowls on every open counter surface we could find with Brian and I wedged in the middle of this gnarly little rib kitchen mixing salad dressing until three a.m. If we were going to keep growing, we needed more room. But given our production schedule, we couldn't devote a lot of time to finding it.

## The Bagel Solution

We knew a guy nearby who had a bagel place, which got our attention because they closed at four p.m., not ten p.m. Also, the kitchen smelled like cinnamon-raisin bagels and not pork ribs. We called the guy and told him our dilemma. He was super chill and said we could use the place until two a.m. when his crew arrived to make bagels, as long as it was spotless when his crew came in for their production shift. Now we had two locations. We could start the manufacturing process at the bagel place during relatively normal working hours, and whatever we couldn't get done for the day's production requirements, we would move to the rib restaurant in the middle of the night and finish there.

There was a small hitch: our manufacturing license wasn't for the bagel place, it was for The Rolling Bones. Could we keep the bagel place secret while still also using The Rolling Bones? Fuck it, we needed to take the risk. It was either grow or die.

To attempt to cover our tracks at the bagel place, we decided to take giant sheets of brown butcher paper and cover all the windows so no one would know what we were doing. In retrospect, we were probably bringing more attention to ourselves by taping up the windows at 4:30 p.m. but we had to do something.

This plan actually worked for a couple of weeks, and it was amazing to start making dressing while the sun was up, but it turned out to be way sketchier than The Rolling Bones because people saw us walking into the bagel restaurant and started asking questions. We ignored the potential issues with the bagel location because we started growing aggressively. Two locations allowed us to make significantly more dressing, which meant we were selling significantly more dressing.

And besides, we had other pressing problems.

We had outgrown the option of storing supplies in the basement of my townhouse and had to rent a storage unit to hold all the olive oil and equipment. At first, it wasn't weird at all: You go to a storage unit and you put stuff in it, enough said. But then we needed to start buying oil in fifty-five-gallon drums instead of little two- or three-liter containers. This was creating all kinds of issues. We were drawing attention to ourselves by purchasing every container of olive oil in our local Sam's Club every week. The day I walked into Sam's Club and bought two pallets of olive oil—that's 780 two-liter bottles of olive oil—the woman at the checkout looked at me with a weird stank eye. "What in the hell are you doin' with all that oil? Some sort of bikini wrestling match?"

I laughed. And lied. "We fry chicken in it." She didn't look convinced, and I knew we couldn't keep buying our supplies from ordinary retail stores. How do large companies buy raw materials? They buy in bulk and ship it to their loading docks. Our storage unit had a loading dock, which meant we were technically just like a big company. So, we started ordering bulk materials. And quickly hit our next challenge.

## Are You Dock High?

Our first bulk order was olive oil in fifty-five-gallon drums. The driver called and asked us to meet him outside at our storage unit. We walked out expecting something like an Amazon delivery van was going to pull up when an 18-wheeler stopped in front of us. "HOLY FUCK" I said. Brian and Matt started laughing in disbelief. The truck driver got out. "Where is the loading dock?" We pointed to the side of the storage unit. He gave us a weird eyebrow movement and didn't look convinced. "Is it dock high?"

We had no idea what that meant, so we just nodded. But he kept asking. "It's dock high? This thing is dock high? I ain't never seen a storage unit facility that was dock high."

Completely baffled by the foreign language he was speaking, we all just kept shaking our heads yes. Hesitantly, the driver got back in his truck and pulled around to the loading dock to find . . . it sure as hell "ain't dock high!"

There was an approximate three-foot gap between our storage unit—the dock—and the back of the truck. We were about three feet short of "dock high." Not happy about how stupid we were, the driver then asked, "Y'all got a dock plate?"

At this point, we couldn't lie anymore. "We have no idea what you are talking about . . . what is a dock plate?" I said. The truck driver was not amused. "A dock plate is the metal you put in between the loading dock and the truck so you can move the product over that little gap into your building. I can't get the product into the building without a dock plate."

Now that I understood that a "dock plate" was essentially a bridge, I told the driver I would be right back and sprinted to the guy at the front desk and asked him if he had a dock plate. He also didn't know what I was talking about and shook his head no. I ran around the inside of the building looking for something metal and found a door that looked heavy duty. I ran back to the driver and said, "How about a steel door?" He told us it was either that or he was leaving, "I got shit to do, boys, and I can't be fucking around with this bullshit."

I ran inside, unscrewed the door, and carried it over. It was the right length, but the width was just barely adequate. There was no room for error. And that wasn't even our biggest problem. We had a major issue with the thickness of the door. It was about two inches thick, which meant we had to jump the two-inch lip to get the pallet onto our makeshift dock plate. As we were setting this physics experiment up, the driver was losing patience. "I ain't fucking with this, you boys got it?" We looked at each other and said, "Sure! We got this. How hard could it be?"

Brian and I jumped into the back of the truck and Matt held the door/dock plate on the other side so it didn't slide away. Brian and I began to push the pallet . . . it weighed as much as a car. Each drum weighed 500 pounds, and there were four of them. As we pushed the pallet up to the door, we just stopped. The thickness of the door was too high. We couldn't just roll the pallet onto our makeshift dock plate and into our storage unit, and couldn't get the pallet to jump that two inches. So we backed up and tried quickly pushing it, hoping the momentum would pop the pallet onto the door. But it was like running into a brick wall over and over.

I looked at Brian and said, "We are going to have to *Cool Runnings* bobsled this motherfucker onto the door."

He started laughing hysterically at my movie reference. We backed up and started pushing it like it was a Jamaican bobsled as fast as we could, but we still couldn't get the pallet onto the door. It was a dead stop.

The good news is that our bobsled efforts were creating just enough damage to help us. Each time we shoved the pallet forward, we were crushing the lip of the door. It looked like we could potentially use the damage to the lip of the door as a ramp if we pushed it hard enough.

At this point, the truck driver was so amused by our spectacle that he stopped complaining about his wasted time and started laughing at our insane and ignorant predicament. And we didn't disappoint our audience. We started the *Cool Runnings* hype chant: "Feel the rhythm, feel the ride, come on, boys, it's bobsled time . . . coooooollllll runn-nnninnnnnggggssssss!" And we took off. We pushed the pallet of oil as hard and as fast as we could from inside the truck and popped the pallet on the door.

"YEEESSSSSSSSSSSSS!" Everyone screamed with celebration, even the truck driver, who was now hysterically laughing at how stupid we were. "FUCK YEAH, BOYS, this is nuts!"

Step 1 was complete. Now we had to get the oil to the loading dock. Slowly, we walked it down our improvised dock plate. And then we heard the "clunk." The metal door began to give way. We jumped down and assessed the situation. The wheels of the pallet jack had sunk into the door from the weight, and the door had begun to buckle in the middle. The pallet of oil was balancing on the door like a tightrope walker in a windstorm.

The truck driver was no help. Now that the oil was off the truck and onto our door/dock plate, it was our liability, not his. So, if the oil fell off the door and exploded, not only were we fucked from a cash standpoint, but we were going to have an environmental disaster on our hands. We needed to make a decision quickly before the oil toppled over, and the only thing we could come up with was to "linebacker hit" the pallet onto the loading dock. The truck driver was now watching our stunts like he was at the circus. Brian and I got into the truck and moved as far back as we could, took off running, and attacked this pallet like an NFL linebacker on a goal line stand. We popped the pallet onto the loading dock, and nothing exploded. "IT WORKED! YESSSSSSSSSSS!" It was a small miracle. We were jumping and high-fiving like we had just won the Super Bowl. The door was completely destroyed. The driver couldn't stop laughing. We had spent about an hour getting this pallet off this truck. We were drenched in sweat, but the oil had made it. Then we looked at each other and said, "Holy shit! All of this for one pallet? We need to figure out a better way."

The driver just laughed as he climbed back into the cab of his truck. "Just tell 'em you don't have a loading dock, and they will bring a truck with an automatic lift gate. Like you see on moving trucks."

That was all we had to do? Just fucking tell them we didn't have a loading dock? Holy shit. You live and you learn. But we needed to stop being so fucking stupid and start picking and choosing the times when we faked it and the times we were honest and told them we don't know shit.

## Moving a Civic

We calculated that by buying the oil in fifty-five-gallon drums, we could eliminate about two hours of work a day and save money on the price per gallon of oil. Seemed genius. But we didn't take into account the weight of these drums of oil. They were like moving around a car. So how the fuck do you get fifty-five-gallon drums into The Rolling Bones or the bagel place without people noticing? How were we going to get these oil drums into a vehicle?

We Googled "rent big truck." Penske was the first to pop up, and they had trucks as large as a thirty-foot box truck. I called to see what type of commercial license we needed to drive these types of gigantic vehicles. "None, just need a driver's license." I made him repeat it. "Yup, just a driver's license," said the Penske worker. Shocked, I quickly ordered the biggest truck they had—"I'll take the thirty-foot box truck with a lift gate, please." We all drove up to the Penske rental place in Baltimore to see what was actually going to happen when one of us tried to drive a thirty-foot box truck. But it was relatively simple. We took it for a couple of laps in the parking lot to get a feel for the size and how to use the mirrors and then drove away, confident truck drivers.

Brian and Matt both had their own cars to protect me as we drove, and we kept our cell phones on so they could tell me if I was going to run off the road. But all in all, it was relatively simple. And as I drove this massive truck down the road with my brothers protecting my path, it felt like we were actually doing it. We were solving problems and finding ways to make our journey work regardless of the fear that came with the solution. And the greatest part of the truck was the lift gate. It was fucking awesome. What an advancement in modern mechanical engineering. We could take a pallet jack and load it up, roll all our shit onto the lift gate, press a button, and rise up to the truck bed like we were levitating dressing gods. Marvelous! Getting our fifty-five-gallon oil drum onto a vehicle problem had been solved. But it didn't solve the five steps you had to climb to get into The Rolling Bones or the fact that we had to lug bright green oil drums into the (not our manufacturing licensed) bagel place in broad daylight.

## Cakes by Patience

We needed another certified kitchen that was easier to operate out of during normal hours. We started searching and found a defunct bakery in a not-very-upscale neighborhood called Cakes by Patience. Her name was Patience, and her dream of selling high-end cakes in the 'hood didn't pan out as a viable business strategy, so she was renting her certified kitchen space by the hour. We rented the building for a day to see how things would work.

Now that we had three kitchens and three storage units, we needed more people we could trust to help us secretly make salad dressing. We called a couple of dudes we went to high school with from Annapolis Gardens, which was subsidized housing. Brian was an honorary member of their (real) gang, and he pitched them to come on as workers. "We'll pay you cash at the end of every day, and you can't tell anyone what you're doing." They all laughed and said, "We got you, Vetter. When do we start?"

We picked half the guys up in the Penske box truck and put straps in the back so they could hold on. We gave Brian's closest friend in the crew, Darren, my mom's suburban to pick up more people. It was not the kind of car that you generally saw in that neighborhood. A few days later, a buddy of mine (who was a cop) called me. "I'm driving behind your mom's suburban and pull up to say 'hi,' and there are eight Black dudes in it. Are you good?" I started laughing hysterically. "Yeah, man. It's Darren. He's helping us make salad dressing with the Annapolis Gardens crew." My buddy replied, "You boys are the craziest motherfuckers I have ever met in my life."

As we pulled into Cakes by Patience with an entire day ahead of us, it felt like we were finally making some progress. We began to unload the supplies into the kitchen, and then the fifty-five-gallon drums arrived. We had a handcart to lower the fifty-five-gallon drum down a single step into Cakes by Patience—which was much easier than dragging 500 pounds *up* the five steps at The Rolling Bones. But not, we discovered, problem-free. As we put the fifty-five-gallon drum on the handcart and tilted it back to move, the tires of the handcart completely flattened. I don't know if you have ever used a handcart without tires, but it doesn't really work. Moving the drums with flat handcart tires was like dragging a Honda Civic with the emergency brake on, but we managed. It was a small hiccup considering what we had overcome with the dock plate, so we moved on with high spirits. Everything was unloaded, and we started to prep for the day's production. As we moved over to get the oil out of the drum to start making the dressing, we realized one critical step we had overlooked. "How the fuck do you get oil OUT OF THE DRUM!"

## Oil Out

You can't tip the drum over with any type of control to pour it out. So how in the hell are we going to get all of this oil out? We scoured Google to figure it out. Apparently, we needed a "drum pump," which was not readily available and very expensive, so we decided to try to recreate it from parts purchased at Home Depot. We bought a hose attachment designed to move water from one area to another as our first attempt and bought a hand pump as backup. The hand pump was very cheap, and we were hoping we wouldn't have to use it. It was basically a sucking version of a salad spinner.

Once the hose solution was in place, Matt took over the Cakes by Patience location, and I got into the truck and headed to The Rolling Bones and the bagel place. But Matt called me an hour later, very frustrated. "This isn't fucking working. The oil is too thick, and it's sucking the hoses closed. I'm fucking leaving. We are paying these people to stand around, and it's a waste of money and time."

I told him to hold tight and I would head to Home Depot and see if we could find a better solution. I found a heavier-duty water pump for a boat and brought it back. It looked good and made sense, and it temporarily made Matt think it COULD work. But he called again, even more mad than before. "THIS ISNT FUCKING WORKING!"

Brian and I made the theme of Matt's journey: figure it out. We would tell him to ask questions, and then our answer would be: Figure it out. But he wasn't figuring it out, and I was trying to make dressing in two different locations, so I was getting annoyed that he hadn't figured it out. I told him to pay the people for the day and have Darren drive everyone home, but HE had to stay there until he figured it out. He was not happy, but hey, all is fair in love and salad dressing. By about eleven p.m., I had received multiple hate texts from him and still no victory message. Concerned about him breaking and going on a shooting spree, I headed down to Cakes by Patience to figure out what was going on.

I walked into a dark room with the noise of a squeaking pump, almost like a rickety rocking chair. And Matt standing in the corner overtop of this drum with his back to me. His arm was slowly moving up and down like he was jerking off, and I could almost hear him whimpering. I walked up and said, "Matt . . . buddy . . . you good?" All of the hose solutions had failed, and he had been trying to hand pump the oil out of the drum for over an hour, with little to show for it. "NO, I'M NOT FUCKING GOOD! I'm sitting here with this stupid fucking hand pump squirting out a fucking ounce every ten minutes in a fucking shit hole called Cakes by Patience. Who the fuck is named Patience? Who?! This is fucking bullshit. I fucking hate this shit! WHAT THE FUCK ARE WE DOING?! FUCK SALAD DRESSING!"

I started hysterically laughing. He kind of laughed but was still super pissed, and I told him we would just go home for the night and figure it out later. We came back the next morning with a couple of "MacGyver" solutions that got the oil out way faster than his hand pump, and that solution held strong for a couple of weeks.

But staying in three little locations with three storage units and no loading dock was the most inefficient thing anyone could ever think of, ever. Every morning we would go to the storage unit, load everything up in the truck by drop off location, go pick up people, drive to the locations, set up shop for the day, and then make dressing. And then, at the end of the night, break everything down, drop everyone off, clean all the equipment, and do the same thing the next day. We needed something more efficient, or Matt was going to have a mental breakdown.

I called Robert, the restaurateur, and told him my predicament. He said he had an unoccupied retail space next door to his restaurant that had a back door that was directly next to his back door. We could store some of the raw materials there so we didn't have to load up The Rolling Bones portion of the materials into the Penske truck, and people could just show up and work. It would make things a little easier. It made sense, and we were searching for any solution that was slightly better than what we were doing. We went with Robert and took a look at the location and thought it was a great idea. We told him we would start moving stuff into the room later that day for storage.

But I had a different plan forming in my mind.

What if we built a kitchen space in the completely open unoccupied retail space next to The Rolling Bones? We could be seen going into The Rolling Bones and then do all the major work next door, and no one would ever know. It was sketchy but could work. We just had to keep the lights off and work in silence (ha!) Who the fuck was going to look in an empty retail location that Robert was going to potentially, maybe someday, rent out?

We obviously didn't tell Robert any of this because he would have said: "No, that's fucking stupid, and illegal, and you will take me down with you." We just took the chance anyway. I always believed it was better to ask for forgiveness than permission or, like in the immortal words of Dave Chappelle about his friend Chip, "I'm sorry, officer, I didn't know I couldn't do that."

## Welcome to the House of Tarps

In retrospect, we should have just set up a meth lab. We would have made way more money, and the sketch factor would have been exactly the same. The new kitchen space consisted of tarps and Rubbermaid tables. We created a little tarp box. Tarps on the floor, walls, and ceilings so nothing could get into the product, tables kept the tarps on the floor down, and the hanging tarps for walls also gave us a little cover in case someone (like Robert!) randomly walked in. We stacked all the other raw materials in front of the tarp walls so it wasn't easy to get to our production area, and we began cranking out dressing.

I personally thought it was a great idea, but Matt was not comfortable with this level of sketch. I realized just how uncomfortable when I got a call from my dad one afternoon while I was at my day job hustling insurance to meet them down at The Rolling Bones. Now, in my dad's defense, this was the first time he had ever seen this sketchy setup that looked like a meth lab. He was pissed because it appeared Matt was about to break. "What the fuck is going on here, Greg? This is fucking insane. Your brother is going to go to jail!" Matt wasn't saying anything and was distancing himself from me while looking at the ground. I went into aggression mode. "What the fuck are you talking about?" I replied.

My dad was slightly confused by my response but didn't back off. "This is a shit show you have going on here!" my dad yelled. I responded, "First off, why the fuck are you here? Secondly, this is just temporary. Everything is fine, our manufacturing license is next door, no one knows we are here, and if Matt hadn't called you, you wouldn't have known either, so why don't you just calm the fuck down."

Matt said nothing. But my dad was right. We needed to get the fuck out of there and streamline our manufacturing situation. The multiple locations and storage units were too much to handle, and eventually, our amazing run of salad dressing gypsies was going to stall out. We started calling real estate friends and found a giant warehouse in a remote part of town that would be perfect for our manmade, meth-style tarp kitchen. Things were looking up until we got a call from the storage unit manager. There was oil everywhere.

"Excuse me?" I said, hoping it wasn't what I thought he was implying. But it was. "Sir, there is about an inch of oil on the floor near your storage unit, and since I know you all make salad dressing, I'm guessing it's coming from your unit. I would get down here immediately."

## Oh, Fuck

Matt and I drove down there, and he was right. A fifty-five-gallon drum had tipped over in the storage unit and completely emptied onto the floor. My heart sank, and panic filled my mind. Was this the end? Were we going to be found out? I didn't even know if we had done anything wrong, but I knew we had to clean up the mess quickly. Fifty-five gallons may not seem like a lot of oil to you, but I want you to imagine spilling one gallon of milk. It covers a lot of ground. Now make it thick and slippery and impossible to get up. That's what we were dealing with. We didn't even know where to start. We tried absorbing it with towels. That didn't work. We tried snow shoveling it out of the door, which kind of helped but didn't clean the floor. The only thing we could think of was kitty litter. We drove to PetSmart to see what we could find. "Excuse me, what is your most absorbent kitty litter?" we asked. "How big is your cat?" the clerk replied. "We have multiple cats, and they are all very big.

They pee a lot and we need the most absorbent kitty litter you make." We walked out of there with the clerks looking very confused and 400 pounds of kitty litter. But the kitty litter worked. We spread it everywhere, and it took care of most of the problem. It was still a little slick, but it was the best we could do. We decided after the kitty litter *pickup* that we were no longer using storage units. We started mapping out our next move.

But the oil spill was the last straw for Matt. He couldn't take the bullshit anymore and called a family meeting.

## Denver

"I'm moving to Denver," Matt said.

We were at my parent's house—the three brothers at the table, my mom and dad sitting to the side. They already knew what Matt was going to say. This meeting was to break it to myself and Brian.

Shocked, Brian and I didn't say anything for a while. We just looked at each other, trying to figure out if Matt was serious or not. Finally, I broke the silence. "Why?" Matt looked at me, paused, and thought through the question. I saw his mind going down a thousand different avenues for the most important reason why he was moving, but I don't think he really knew. He eventually started talking and tried making up reasons that would justify the dramatic move out of nowhere but the logic really never came together. Long story short, he was done. He didn't want to be a part of the salad-dressing gypsy shit show any longer.

This was his first job out of college, and he thought the grass was greener on the other side, and maybe it was. Having been from the other side's grass for four, long, cubicle-ridden, cold-calling years, I tried to express to him that the other side's grass fucking sucks. We tried to reason with him, but he didn't want to hear it. Finally, he said he had been talking to a therapist about how unhappy he had been, and the therapist wanted the brothers to come to his office before he left for Denver. I liked the idea and said, "Sure, we would love that, do we get to lie down on a couch like in the movies?" Matt didn't laugh. "The meeting is tomorrow at noon," Matt said.

Brian and I drove to the meeting together and walked into what looked like a hippy's dorm room. A big, tall, very happy guy greeted us as we walked in. William was not an MD but a certified counselor specializing in addicts, grief, and marriages. He had the perfect personality to handle all of that. We all sat down, and William started, "So, how do you feel about Matt moving to Denver?" I explained how we thought he was making a rash decision for a young kid who was dealing with a lot of adversity and that the only reason he thought we were such horrible pieces of shit was because he hadn't had another job to compare it to. We explained how much we loved him and how all we wanted to do was make this business work. Brian chimed in and told him not to do it. The brothers were stronger together, and his move seemed random.

William listened to us go back and forth for about an hour and, at the end, to our surprise, sided with us. His conclusion was that we loved Matt and only wanted to see each other succeed. Matt didn't say anything, and William asked us to leave the office so he could follow up with Matt. As we drove home, Brian and I talked about the chance that William may actually convince Matt to stay.

Matt left the next morning with my mom, and they drove to Denver.

## Field Guide: Lessons Learned

**What You Need to Know**
Not everyone is ready to drink out of a firehose and don't assume that they are.

**How to Do It**
Remember the quote, "When you assume, you make an ass out of you and me." We assumed Matt was prepared for the job and had the bandwidth to "figure it out." Not everyone is you, and not everyone cares the way you care. Understanding someone's capabilities as they are at that exact moment is very important to keeping people engaged and methodically growing. Be patient and strategically improvise. If you thought someone could handle a big job and they cannot, then decide if they can do a different job that requires less effort. OR, give them more support and training. We were very quick to say, "They don't have it," but in reality, we didn't provide the training for them to thrive. There are multiple stages of this theory and the opposite of this is just as bad. We have given people too much time and too much training and they still couldn't do the job. There is a very intricate balance of capabilities, capacity, training, and environment. They all must be analyzed and reanalyzed constantly.

**What You Need to Know**
When you get to the end of your rope, tie a knot and hang on. It will always look different in the morning.

**How to Do It**
The days were insane in the beginning, and there were moments that felt like everything was over. When that happens, take the rest of the day off and find perspective. Read books about great people who did great things so you can put your minuscule

problems into historical perspective. Take a long walk in nature and think. Watch a funny movie. Go see your kids play sports. Go spend time with your pet. All of these little areas will change your perspective on the current problem that's occupying your mind. In addition, you will probably come up with the solution to your problem by removing yourself from the negativity of it all.

### What You Need to Know
When evaluating a new venture, look for: Easily scalable + Good return on time + Fun.

### How to Do It
This formula runs in complete contradiction to many VC books about building a moat around your business so you can fend off competition in regard to "easily scalable." And maybe they are right for building billion-dollar unicorns. I define "easily scalable" as: the process exists and can be implemented without having to invent anything insane. Finally, this business will take every waking moment, so it better be fun.

# FOUR

I admit, I was shocked when Matt drove off to Denver. How hadn't Brian and I convinced him to stay? I was sure he'd stick around after we all met with Counselor Will. Then: Taillights.

But Brian and I didn't miss a beat. If Matt was out, we were still 100 percent in. And we were beginning to adapt our roles and our strategies to keep the business growing.

Instead of doing demos and hand-selling product in stores, Brian turned into our temporary production manager. We also needed more consistent help if Matt wasn't going to be around. One of the people we reached out to was one of Matt's friends—a guy named Richard, who was really into consumer packaged goods (CPG). Why? Honestly, I have no idea. But he was obsessed with anything brand related and was always checking in with us. So, we called him to see if he wanted to help with in-store demos because Brian was going to be focused on making all the salad dressing.

Richard immediately said yes. We all met and explained what he had to do. The job was this: Go into the natural foods chain location, set up a demo, put on a smile, say you are part of the family, and sell the shit out of the dressing. Seemed easy enough, and this guy was fucking pumped. Probably a little too pumped, when we think back on the moment. But we needed the help, and he was enthusiastic. We decided to give him a try. Brian and I met him on a Saturday morning at a coffee shop to get caffeinated, and then Brian and Richard were going to drive to the Bethesda store together.

Standing in stores and handing out samples seems easy until you walk into the chaos of a grocery store on a Saturday, and no one wants to even look at you. All the shoppers are there to shop and have potential interest in what you have to sell. But they look at you like you are a homeless guy at a stoplight begging for money. Most young adults are not ready for that level of social anxiety, and so the number of people who could actually hit our target of twenty bottles an hour was very low. But we had high hopes for Richard because he was so gung ho.

Richard was already at the coffee shop on his second cup of coffee when we arrived. He was sitting at a table with his foot bouncing off the ground a million miles an hour, with eyeballs as big as saucers. This dude was juiced up. We went over the expectations, and then Brian and Richard headed for the store.

It didn't take long for the situation to unravel.

About thirty minutes after we parted at the coffee shop, Brian called me. Richard's energy was rapidly escalating from pumped to volcanic, said Brian. "He's in the front seat bouncing around like he's on cocaine, telling me about how he is going to dominate this demo, and the next thing I know, he is yelling at me to pull the car over!" While Richard puked by the side of the road, Brian told me he was considering leaving him there rather than risk Richard ruining his car upholstery. I told Brian in no uncertain terms that he could not leave Richard—our brother's friend—by the side of the road. We did agree, however, that when Richard stopped puking, we should not put him in the store doing demos. Brian drove Richard back to his car.

The next day, I tried to harness Richard's untamed energy in another way. I called him to ask if he could help with making the dressing—since maybe demos were not his thing. This was the first time we brought an "outsider" into our handmade bottling operation—apart from family and Brian's gang member buddies from Annapolis Gardens. So, we had to make it very clear to him that if he told anyone what we were doing, we would have to kill him. We were kidding—mostly. But we needed to set the tone for him. This was not a game. This was serious business.

We put Richard on the easiest job we had, which was Capper. After the bottle was filled, you needed to screw on a cap. Not complicated stuff. But an hour into production, Richard was making some weird noises, and bottles were backing up at the capping section of our assembly line.

I approached Richard. "What's going on, man? Why aren't you capping?" Shaking his hands like he had just picked up something hot, he opened his right palm, and his hand was bleeding near his thumb crease from turning the caps. "I have to leave, man. I can't do this with my right hand. It's bleeding now and really hurts."

I stood there stunned for a moment, wondering if he was fucking with me. He wasn't. So, I made a suggestion. "Why don't you use your left hand?"

Common sense, right? But for Richard, it was like I'd switched on the lights in a dark room. "Yes! I will do that!"

Then I went a step further into Common Sense Land. "And why don't you use these gloves with grips on the palms so you don't hurt your hands?" Richard looked over at the other Capper right next to him—who was wearing gloves. "Yes! I should have done that!"

Richard ended up working with us for several years. And he was always 100 percent effort, and zero percent common sense, which taught me a leadership lesson: It can take some time and exploration to find out where someone needs to be within the company to do their best work.

## Warehouse #1

Now we wanted to get everything out of the storage units and move into our new temporary tarp kitchen in the warehouse on the outskirts of town. We mapped out how we were going to run the business now that we had a single location and divided up the daily responsibilities for production. Brian would be the mixer, I was the filler and production conductor, and we would fill in the rest of the production line with guys we could trust.

We loaded everything into the Penske truck and moved into the new warehouse where we were secretly building our tarp kitchen. It was pretty awesome to have everything in one location. All the raw materials, all the equipment, all the people, a LOADING DOCK that was DOCK HIGH! It was also pretty close to the Annapolis Gardens housing project, so we were able to hire a few of the guys we knew, and they could walk to work.

Being so close to Annapolis Gardens was a good thing and a bad thing. On the one hand, our guys were never late to work. On the other hand, they were a bit too comfortable working in their own neighborhood. When the guys would take a cigarette break, they might decide to walk back to their regular neighborhood spot and start smoking weed.

I wasn't too concerned that they were getting too high. But I was pretty worried when I saw a pack of ten dudes, all smoking blunts, making their way back from break to my warehouse. That's not really keeping a low profile. So, we had to make a rule around their cigarette breaks: If you want to smoke weed, go back to your homes and do it inside. And PLEASE don't walk back to the warehouse in a giant group while finishing your blunts. They all laughed and agreed.

Getting to work in the new building was bittersweet because Matt wasn't there to experience how efficient things COULD be. But that seems to be life in a nutshell. My many mantras rang in my head.

"It's always darkest before dawn..."

"We are always three feet from gold..."

"When you get to the end of your rope, tie a knot and hang on..."

Life usually works out in your favor if you can find a way to endure the tough times, but you have to live those experiences to understand that lesson. After Matt left for Denver, I realized how hard it was to build a brand without cutting corners. If we had just hired a co-packer and made a mediocre product, Matt wouldn't be in Denver, and we wouldn't be in a sketchy warehouse with a tarp kitchen. But here we were, acting like a bunch of "meth gypsies" trying to scale a handmade salad dressing in the natural foods chain. Salad dressing. All of this for fucking salad dressing?

I knew it wasn't about the salad dressing. It was about seeing if we could change our stars and do the things that people said couldn't be done. I obviously didn't want to ruin my relationship with my brother, but I also knew we had to find the edge of what was possible at that stage of our journey and then adjust accordingly. Finding that limit is what determines who survives and who doesn't.

## Surprise Visitors

Turns out, the sketchy warehouse location with the tarp kitchen didn't last long. One day around lunch time, we were in full operations mode with Brian mixing dressing in head-to-toe Helly Hansen ocean gear so he didn't get drenched with olive oil. I was the coxswain of two makeshift hand-bottling lines, yelling out orders and encouragement, making sure everyone was moving quickly, and replenishing bottles in both lines while packing boxes. When into this hub of activity walks a real estate broker, trailed by two clients who were considering renting this warehouse. Which was *not* supposed to have a salad manufacturing operation in it.

The three, dressed in business casual attire, walked in. And everybody froze. Every head on our production line turned to look at the newcomers. They half-smiled at us. And no one said a word. The broker said he was showing the warehouse portion of the space to some potential tenants. We just kept staring at them. They slowly backed out of the room and left.

No one said anything for about a minute, and then Brian and I looked at each other, and silently, with only our eyes, told each other we were packing up that location at the end of the day and never going back. The gypsies were on the run again. We finished bottling the dressing that had already been made, packed everything into the Penske, and left for good.

## Warehouse #2

I needed to find a real manufacturing location, and the gypsy life needed to stop. I started looking for a manufacturing space like my life depended on it—because it did. There wasn't much move-in ready manufacturing space in the size we needed. There were huge buildings or tiny kitchens, but nothing in between. We finally found space in Millersville, which was twenty-five minutes from my house. The new location was even better than the previous one. It was new, had plenty of room for trucks to pull up and turn around, and was in a really nice area. But once there, we were taking no chances and went back to making the dressing at night so no one would walk through the building in the middle of the day and quiz us about our manufacturing license.

We continued to sell the shit out of the product, and by this point, we were in eighteen natural foods locations. We were cranking product off the shelves, and we were buying more raw materials than ever before—including a giant oil shipment coming to the new storage facility in fifty-five-gallon drums. With so much room, we could order anything we wanted now without worry. So, when our delivery truck pulled up, we directed the driver to the back of the building and went to get the dock plate.

It wasn't there.

We had left it in the old warehouse when we were packing up in the middle of the night like the Baltimore Colts.

No dock plate?! Again?! Fuck.

But we had learned a few tricks since we started driving the Penske truck. We told the 18-wheeler to pull up, dead center in the middle of the parking lot, and we would back our truck up to his truck with our lift gate as a bridge. The driver's truck was packed, so there wasn't enough room for us to get in and get a legitimate running start to jump the gap to the lift gate of our truck. We needed gravity to help us, so we made our lift gate a couple of inches lower than the truck's trailer. Then we planned to make our fifty-five-gallon delivery fall onto our truck.

We explained what we were going to do to the driver, and he loved it. He started hysterically laughing. "This is the craziest fucking thing I've ever seen on a drop-off. You boys are wild as hell!" We laughed and told him about the storage unit story, and said, "This is nothing. We got this jump all day."

Brian and I got behind the pallet jack, put our feet against the existing cargo in the truck, pushed off as hard as we could, and took off running. We had about six feet of runway to gain speed and jump the gap. We hit the end of the truck's trailer and TAKE OFF! We were fucking Elliott and ET soaring through the air. The oil made it on our truck without a dock plate, and the truck driver was cheering us on like we were horses at the Kentucky Derby.

We had three more pallets to go. But we successfully got them all off the truck. It was hilarious and much easier than that first day. We gave the driver some bottles of dressing and told him to keep an eye out for us one day. "We are going to be big!" He laughed and replied,

"I ain't never seen a bunch of young dudes so pumped up on salad dressing. Good luck to ya."

Even as we enjoyed that moment, we were at a critical juncture. Our path ahead was not yet clear. This phase of the journey is when most people break. There is just too much chaotic uncertainty without any substantial reward, and the solutions to your problems are more difficult than the problem itself. Yes, there is opportunity to be seized. But to do it, you must go through what Joseph Campbell called the "Hero's Journey." It is not for the faint of heart and will test every ounce of your testicular fortitude.

And our testicles were about to be tested.

## Field Guide: Lessons Learned

### What You Need to Know
Never stop moving forward.

### How to Do It
The first key is to remember where you are going and why. Then set reminders in your journal, your whiteboard, your mirror, your car . . . to never stop moving forward. Find a quote that inspires you to keep pressing on and put it everywhere. Play a game with yourself to see how resilient you are when something comes up you feel you can't deal with. Can this problem or obstacle break me? Or can I solve it while remaining positive? Can I view this as a test that needs to be passed so I can move on to the next level of this video game called my life? Most people are going to think you are insane, and that's OK. This is about you setting the pace and moving forward toward your goal no matter what.

### What You Need to Know
Prepare to win the day . . . every morning.

### How to Do It
If you could get a head start for a race that had the biggest prize in the world for winning, wouldn't you do it? That's the morning preparation process. No one does it, and it's the differentiator for getting the most out of your day. Map out what is in store for you that day by hour and by objective. What is critical and urgent versus important and beneficial? What moves you forward toward your goal versus what does nothing for your forward progress? Write all of that down and let it be your compass for the day. At the end of the day, review it and see where you ended up. Don't change your goal if it gets hard, just keep recalibrating until you accomplish it.

### What You Need to Know
Keep an unreal sense of urgency.

### How to Do It
Creating urgency is only effective if everyone is running at the same pace and toward the same goal. Figure out what the goal is and make it easily digestible so everyone can work toward the same thing with very simple instructions. That will allow everyone to move faster. We knew the only way we were going to get out of the sketchy environment we were in was to sell more bottles. That was the goal. Then we needed to figure out how to sell as many bottles as possible as quickly as possible. That simply came down to doing demos in good stores and making enough bottles to support the stores that we were demoing in. Every other detail in our business fell into those buckets. Does this help us do demos? Does this allow us to make dressing more efficiently?

# FIVE

We had found a nice little rhythm to the tarp space we were in but still needed a full-time location. It was a time-consuming hunt. I was calling everybody under the sun, but I still wasn't making much progress.

That's when a more pressing crisis popped up on my dashboard.

I got a call that our drum pump had broken. We had no way of getting the oil out of the barrels without it. I headed to the warehouse to see if we could figure it out. I couldn't. We called the manufacturer, and they said it was going to be at least two weeks before they could get us any replacement machinery. We called every store that sold drum pumps—same answer.

## Drum Tipping

After about two days of this, I started getting frustrated, and my brain shifted into MacGyver mode. There had to be a creative solution to our problem. Couldn't we just use gravity? We were out of options, so gravity it was. We waited until all our neighbors in the industrial complex had left, and we attempted our gravity test. We wheeled down an empty plastic fifty-five-gallon barrel—one that had no lid and wheels so we could easily move it around. We positioned the full fifty-five-gallon drum at the edge of the loading dock. Our plan was to tip the full drum, braced by the loading dock, and catch the oil stream in our empty plastic barrel.

All of this made sense in my head. Brian was positioned down low to catch the oil. I was going to tip the fifty-five-gallon drum over and then open the drum. By my very (un)scientific calculations, this was a solid plan. Step 1: tip the drum over. This thing was fucking heavy, and we were trying to ease it down, but the minute we began to tip it over, we lost control, and it just fell with a thud. But it landed pretty close to where we had planned to position it. So, we moved forward. We put the empty barrel in place, and I prepared to open the now-angled full drum.

"Welp, here we go," I said. "Battle Stations!"

I turned open the spout on the drum with a wrench.

Oil shot into the back of the plastic drum, knocking it over on its side. Fifty-five gallons of olive oil gushed into the parking lot like a greasy tsunami.

We scrambled to save the oil from being wasted, but it couldn't be done. We couldn't get the empty drum off the ground because the oil was pouring all over it, and by the time we were able to move the full drum, it was too late. We looked like a bunch of guys who just competed in an olive oil wrestling match. But that wasn't even the worst of it. What we didn't notice at the time (because it was the middle of the night) was how bad the parking lot looked. We came in the next day, greeted by a black path of dirty oil from our loading dock into a drain in the middle of the parking lot. I knew right away we had a big problem. If someone were to see this (and it was hard to miss), they might report us to the state, and the authorities would find out we were not manufacturing in the space for which we had a license. We'd be lucky if all we got was a fine. We'd be lucky if we survived at all!

I called a power wash company to come power wash the parking lot, but that didn't help. It looked like absolute shit, with a giant oil stain pointing like a black, slimy arrow directly to our building. The need for our own space or a manufacturing solution was now reaching DEFCON 1, and it was all I could think about.

While doing a demo one Saturday, we ran into a crab salsa company that used a small co-packer in Pennsylvania. The crab salsa guys raved about their partner. "They are wonderful and can do small batch production. We have used them for five years and love them!"

This sounded promising. We called the group and set up an R&D session in their facility to show them how we made it. All the trash we had been talking about co-packers didn't matter at this point because this gypsy life we were living was going to get our business shut down.

We went on a tour of the facility, and they showed us how they make dressing. "And here is all the dehydrated garlic that we can just add water to or it can be thrown directly in your product. And over here is how we make the lemon natural flavor actually taste like lemon."

"What is that?" I asked.

"Oh, that's citric acid. It gives the tartness that a natural lemon would."

I was confused as I looked at the labeling. "Acid? But it says if it gets on your skin to immediately go to a burn washing station."

They responded nonchalantly, "Yup, DO NOT let that get in your eyes or on your skin."

Me, still confused. "But you can eat it?"

Them, still super confident. "You sure can."

That didn't sound logical at all, but we continued on the tour. Afterward, they said they were confident they could make our product. "Not only can we make it, but we can save you money per bottle because you have been making it so inefficiently." After we left, their R&D team found a better way to actually make the product. "We will send you a sample."

The sample arrived, and it tasted pretty close. And it was NOT made in Cakes by Patience or a rib restaurant, so that was a plus. I called the R&D guy, and he explained they changed the way they used the garlic to take into account the dehydrated garlic they were using. Initially, it seemed like it would work. And we had no other option. I mean, we were making it in fucking tarp tent kitchens and bouncing from one crisis to the next. We bought an initial production run of 600 cases, which were shipped to the stores we were in.

Initially, we heard nothing negative. And I was thinking: Holy shit, we did it!

And then, my wife came home with some of the new bottles from the co-packer. And it tasted like garlic ass.

It was horrible. Like actual garlic shit. "OH, FUCK. This shit sucks!"

But we had bought a month's worth for eighteen stores. We needed to sell through it as fast as possible and go back to making it ourselves. Customer service emails started piling up asking why it tasted like garlic ass. We responded with something sweet like: "When you use real ingredients sometimes the flavor is not consistent. We are sorry and love you, so we will give you a free bottle. Please stay with us!"

One woman called and left the nastiest voicemail I have ever received about salad dressing. So, I called her back. "Dianne? This is Greg Vetter with Tessemae's. I received your voicemail." There was dead silence on the other end. Then: "Uhhhhhh . . . I didn't know real people check the messages." I mustered up as much positivity as I could: "Yup, we sure do. This is my cell phone, and my family's life depends on this business working, so we need to make sure every customer is happy."

She didn't say much and just thanked me for calling.

This was in August, and my hunt for manufacturing space went into "Kill for Jesus" mode—that's a saying my dad used to use when we only focused on one thing and every other detail in your life took a back seat. I started looking for anything I could find that would allow us to make dressing efficiently and to scale. And in the midst of this hunt, we also realized we needed a better waxing solution, and our hunt for wax would eventually dovetail with our hunt for manufacturing space.

Our wax process and opening experience sucked compared to the Maker's Mark wax experience we were trying to copy. Their experience was orgasmic: Tab sticking out, soft wax, clean pull, wax stayed on the cap. And the bottle was truly next level. We started calling Maker's Mark to figure out how they did it, but no one ever called us back. Brian decided to take a road trip.

He drove seven hours down to Lebanon County, Kentucky. He walked up to the receptionist and asked for the head of bottling, whose name popped up on Brian's Google search. The guy walked out, a little confused, and asked what he could help Brian with.

"Wax. My brothers and I make salad dressing, and we wax all the bottles just like you. The only problem is our wax sucks, and we need to figure out a better way." The Maker's Mark guy started laughing and replied, "You boys put the wax on the dressings?"

"Yes, sir, we do, and I brought you some."

This was a key part of our process. We had learned that the trick to building something from nothing is approaching it with a "beginner's mind." This allows people to appreciate the struggle and relate to you, which then allows them to put their guard down and help you.

The Maker's Mark guy loved the story so much that he spent the day with Brian and gave us his wax supplier's contact information to start buying wax from them, with Maker's Mark's permission. It was a major success. We called the wax supplier in Illinois and told them the head of bottling at Maker's Mark sent us. Completely shocked, the wax supplier responded, "How in the hell did you get them to let you use their patented wax?" We laughed and told him we were on a mission from God, and Maker's Mark recognized our energy.

And this is where the wax issue dovetails with our search for permanent manufacturing space.

Word got around Lebanon County, Kentucky, that a bunch of crazy brothers were waxing salad dressing bottles, and we got a call from Kentucky's Economic Development Department to see if we wanted to move our business down near Maker's Mark. We were flattered. We didn't really want to move but took the proposal to Maryland to see if they could match it or even come close.

Maryland basically told us to fuck off. So, we started pursuing Kentucky. Everything we asked for, they gave us. Free land, no taxes, support in hiring people. Once we had the formal proposal, we sent it to Maryland again to see if they would match it: "Not interested." We're trying to manufacture in Maryland and you are not interested? No wonder Baltimore is a shit show.

We had a family meeting to discuss moving to Kentucky. No one was really on board except Brian and me, because we had brainwashed ourselves to succeed no matter what. Genevieve was supportive like she always was, but it took a little convincing that we could build a great life in a new state without family nearby (and in the middle of nowhere). We found a cute town thirty minutes from where we would put the plant, and she started getting excited.

I canceled my gym memberships and started to get my affairs in order as we were about to sign the deal with Kentucky. Then one morning, I received a call from a blocked number. But I answered. "Greg, this is the Howard County Executive of Maryland, and I am at the state retreat for economic development. Your name keeps popping up. Are you still going to Kentucky?"

I paused. "Yeah, we are planning on signing the deal Friday."

It was a Monday, and he said to give him the week to make some moves. Tuesday morning, I received a call from his head of economic development saying that she didn't have anything in Howard County, but she wanted to meet for coffee to get an understanding of who we were. We met later that day, and I told her the story up to that point. She was floored. "We are keeping you in Maryland, there is no way we are letting you go to Kentucky." I laughed and told her I was signing the deal on Friday, so she had until then. She called the next morning and told me to meet her in Essex, Maryland.

Now, keep in mind that Essex, Maryland, is in the Bermuda Triangle of shitty fucking Baltimore towns. You have Dundalk, Middle River, and Essex. There is literally a giant poop processing facility on the border of Middle River and Dundalk, and the high schools play the annual Poop Bowl to see who has to claim the poop tower for the following year. A beautiful part of the world . . . really . . . BUT . . .

There was a building that was move-in ready, and she wanted me to see it. I didn't tell anyone about the building and just drove up there. It was a full city block with ten loading docks. I met the real estate group and told them the story, and by the end, the leader of the property group just started laughing, and said, "Make us an offer."

I went home and calculated what I thought we could pay, tiered it out over five years, and sent it to him. It was a long shot, but I had nothing to lose. He called me and said, "If you can give us guarantees that you won't default, the building is yours." What?! 36,000 square feet with refrigeration and drains in the floor? Ours? "What kind of guarantees do you need?" He laid out the amount of money he needed from us to secure the lease, which amounted to basically my dad's house. How confident was I in this business? Was I willing to bet my dad's house on it?

I went to a park in my parents' community that overlooked the water. I sat on a bench that a man had dedicated to his wife, who died of cancer, with an engraved marble slab and a compass. The inscription read: "The voice of nature loudly cries, and many a message from the skies, that something in us never dies." —Robert Burns.

I read the quote over and over again and then looked over the water. A blue heron came up out of the marsh grass and flew right in front of me. That seemed like an omen. I looked up blue heron omens, and they were very good signs of luck and prosperity. I knew what I had to do, and I called my dad for a meeting. We sat on a couch outside of his bedroom, and I explained that the real estate group needed him to guarantee his house for us to get the building, and if we failed and couldn't pay the lease, they would take the home I grew up in.

Without hesitation, he said, "Yes. I am in. And if you fail, we will all move to Colorado and live in trailers together or something."

I gave him a big hug. "Are you sure?" He replied, "That's my final answer." I couldn't believe how much faith he had in me and immediately called the real estate group back and told them we would take the building. It was close by, already done, no one had to move, and we could scale the business. It was a gift from God. I picked up Brian and Genevieve and drove them out to the building. They asked where the fuck we were. I took out a key and opened it. We walked into the back manufacturing area and I said, "This is ours for the next five years. It's time to fill this bitch."

Our manufacturing location problem was solved. A huge weight was lifted from my shoulders. We would live to fight another day. We didn't have to move to Kentucky or waste time building something from scratch. It all just felt right. Except that Matt wasn't with us. He was still in Denver trying to make that life work so that part was still bittersweet. But apparently, word got to him that we were actually "doing it," and he started randomly calling to check in. We would chat like brothers do, but kept it very surface level and cordial.

One day he called and said he wanted to come back to Tessemae's. I wasn't buying it. "Excuse me? Why? You left and went to Denver." So, he went on to explain what had just happened in Kansas City,

(Kansas, not Missouri). Matt couldn't find a job anywhere in Denver outside of a staffing company that ran a "boiler room" sales operation. I knew that was not what Matt pictured when he moved out there, but he had to pay his bills.

So Matt was at the company's training retreat in Kansas City (Kansas), and there weren't many food options for the team after hours. The best they could find were chain restaurants. One night, they ended up at a southwestern grill-style outlet. Matt gave me a play-by-play account. "I ordered my food. As we began to eat, I mumbled to myself, 'I could really use some Tessemae's Lemon Garlic on this shit,'" Matt said. "One of my buddies asked what that was. So, I explained what we had done and that we were growing. How we started our own manufacturing plant now, and you guys were trying to go national with the natural foods chain and how good the dressing was . . . and then I noticed everyone's faces. Twelve people with their jaws wide open and dead silent. And then one guy said, 'SO. WHAT. THE FUCK. ARE. YOU. DOING. HERE?!' I stared back at him, shrugged my shoulders, and said I didn't know."

But it didn't take long for Matt's realization to set in. "So that is why I'm calling. I don't want to be here. I want to come home and work."

I didn't say anything for thirty seconds and then said, "I'll think on it tonight and call you tomorrow morning with my decision."

The next morning, I called with the following demands: "Monday morning at our coffee shop. You will be there at 7:30 a.m. You will work for free until a sixty-day review. You will do everything I ask of you without complaining, and if all of those things happen, we will take you back." There was a pause on Matt's end. "But it's Friday. I'm in Denver. I have a roommate." "None of which is my problem," I told him. "You decide."

Monday morning, I woke up, journaled, went to the gym, and pulled up to the coffee shop. The front is all glass, and as I walked up, I saw Matt all the way in the back—where we used to sit—with an espresso for him and me. A deep feeling of relief washed over my body. The brothers were back and united again. Thank God. We talked and laughed about his roommate's response to the short notice and how he got from Denver to Annapolis so quickly. And then I asked him, "Want to go see the manufacturing facility?"

We got in the car and drove up. He didn't know what to expect. As we walked into the back of this massive building, he was shocked. He just looked around in complete amazement. After about two minutes of silence, he blurted out, "I only needed one loading dock! Not ten."

But now, instead of seeing the problems, Matt could see the future.

## Field Guide: Lessons Learned

### What You Need to Know
There is no trivial comment for the CEO or leader.

### How to Do It
Understand that every action and comment is being processed and analyzed. Staying positive in the face of chaos will dictate how your team reacts to that situation. Remind yourself every morning who you are and what your role is. If you need to speak to someone or vent, find a performance coach, therapist, or friend that you can let out your frustrations to. Don't use your spouse. They are under enough stress from the life you both are currently living. They don't need your daily bullshit as well.

### What You Need to Know
Disarm everyone with kindness.

### How to Do It
My dad always used to say, "You will catch more bees with honey than vinegar." I didn't know what that meant until I needed random strangers to help me solve life-altering obstacles. Don't act like an expert when you are not. Don't be an asshole when you don't need to be. Smile. Have a positive tone in your voice. And begin every conversation with, "I don't know shit about shit, and I really need your help." And then say thank you.

### What You Need to Know
Action creates more action.

### How to Do It
"Leap and the net will appear," a Zen saying. Start right now and begin working on something. It doesn't matter on what, just begin. Then ask for help. See what answers you receive. Some help will be good, some will be bad . . . it doesn't matter. You are trying to get your action going until it turns into momentum. At the beginning of your journey, everything is going to feel wrong, like you know nothing. That could be correct, but you need to keep going. Eventually you will stumble onto some "wins" that will accelerate your trajectory from snail pace to tortoise speed. That's still moving forward. If it is meant to be, it will work.

# SIX

Our new space allowed us to install machinery. Having automated machinery was awesome. Not knowing how to use any of it was not.

We had to keep both of our old hand-filling lines up in case the newly installed machine-bottling line went down, which happened more often than we expected. For about two months, we just kept the old lines up every day and would go back and forth depending on which line was working well that day. It wasn't ideal since we had just spent 300k on automated manufacturing equipment, but we needed to get the orders out on time and having both processes up was the only way we could ensure the dressing got made.

We kept calling people to help us but the only people who knew how to solve these problems were working in manufacturing plants fixing their own issues. A very common response was, "Let me see if I can get out there later in the week, things are a little crazy right now." And the "later in the week" never came.

By the grace of God, our new co-packer friends down the street gave us the name of a mechanic that had some spare time and wanted some part-time work. His name was Frank, and he was about sixty, short, muscular, but with a beer belly, and a reputation for being able to fix anything that had parts.

Frank the Fixer wore faded Lee jeans that he had broken in through hard work, a faded light blue short-sleeve shirt with his name on it (that he made himself) that was always tucked in, and cowboy boots that carried a pistol. He was a classic manufacturing silver fox, who rocked a perfectly manicured mustache and a big smile. He took a look at our machines and then gave us a description of what was happening and why.

We kept asking questions that only idiots would ask and he finally said, "Boys, this thing ain't got no feelings. It's not a person. You just find the problem and ya fix it. Simple as that."

So, what was our problem? Frank knew. "Y'all don't have a preventative maintenance plan. You just let the machine work until it don't. Then try to fix it quickly when it's down. That's real dumb."

Frank went on to explain that we needed a full-time mechanic who had an inventory of backup parts and followed a preset schedule of preventative maintenance—which meant every day, you check every part on that day's schedule, and if anything isn't perfect, you fix it before it breaks. That way, the bottling line never stops running. That made a lot of sense to us, especially since we were doing the complete opposite, and it wasn't working. We needed a full-time expert watching over the machines so that Matt didn't have to jerk off pistons again for an entire week.

We asked Frank if he knew anyone who could help us full time. He said he would think about it and get back to us. We asked to pay him for his time. He laughed. "You can get me some beer." What kind did he like? "Cold, wet, and free!"

We laughed and thanked him again for stopping by. Until he found someone full time, he would check in at least once a week to make sure everything was running smoothly. Honestly, once he opened our eyes to preventative maintenance, we started thinking that way, and our bottling line started working for longer stretches of time.

Matt was doing a good job running things and learning on the go. He was very dedicated to earning back our trust, but it was obvious that he wanted to get paid. It had been two months of him working fifteen-hour days for nothing. He called for a meeting at the coffee shop to have a sixty-day review. We sat down with our espressos, and he went on to explain why he deserved to be paid. "I'm the first one in the plant at six a.m., I have a good attitude, I'm not getting frustrated, all the orders are going out on time regardless of the obstacles I have to overcome on a daily basis . . ." I listened without emotion. He kept going and going, and I just sat there until he ran out of things to say. When he finally stopped talking, I just stared at him in silence to see what he would do. He grabbed my wallet and phone and jokingly said, "If you don't give me a 30k salary, I'm taking your phone and wallet."

"Done," I said.

"Well, great, that was easy," he said.

We shook on it, and as we walked out, I said, "I had planned on giving you a salary of 60k, but 30k will do."

Matt jumped. "What?! No, I'll take sixty. I'll take sixty."

I smiled. "Nope, you were very adamant about thirty, so thirty it is. We shook on it."

He reluctantly agreed that we shook on it and was grateful he had something.

Matt still needed to learn the ways of non-college life, and we still needed to make him "earn it."

Our demo plan in stores was still working, and we were selling more and more dressing every day. We needed more quality people to make it because we were using both hand-bottling and machine-bottling lines. When you are working in manufacturing and trying to hit productivity goals while simultaneously maintaining the highest form of quality, trust is very important. We turned to our friend Darren.

## Growing through People

Darren was Brian's oldest friend from high school and, unfortunately, had a life that was a typical experience of the 'hood. He got into a bunch of trouble in high school, and my dad was constantly having to vouch for him as a character witness in court. When Darren was facing his final strike, my dad promised the court that he would get Darren into college if they gave him one last chance.

My dad helped him get a scholarship to play lacrosse in college at a D2 school out of state, but Darren turned it down. Very quickly after high school, he impregnated his girlfriend with twins, started selling drugs, and then was "gutted" in a knife fight from his sternum to his belly button. After recovering, he had been bouncing around from job to job, still living in the 'hood, when we saw him working with a road crew in Annapolis. We called him later that day to see if he wanted to make dressing instead of working on the road crew, and he jumped at the offer. It looked like he had finally grown up and was ready to work hard. He was always a wonderful guy but had a tendency toward self-sabotage. We wanted this dressing opportunity to be his chance to get out of his old habits.

After a couple of months of hourly work, we offered him a salaried job as our plant manager. In addition to the salary, Brian owned a beautiful townhouse in Towson with a big yard that he wasn't living in and Darren could move into with his family. Darren's commute would be shorter and he could get out of the 'hood. We gave him the use of my mom's suburban, so he could still pick up guys when he needed to and not worry about getting a car of his own. We just needed him to show up on time and keep the production crew in check. He accepted the job and was very grateful.

My dad always had this belief that people just needed a chance, and if you gave them the opportunity for advancement, they would take it and soar. I had a different view of the world, but always tried to be pleasantly surprised with my dad's level of hope. We told my dad what we had done for Darren, and he was over the moon. Everything was working to the best of our ignorant abilities, and we were progressing according to plan. Matt was working hard and keeping the dressing moving, Darren was keeping all the guys focused and in check, Brian was selling the shit out of it, Genevieve was making sure we weren't going to go to jail, Frank was stopping by weekly to make sure we weren't doing anything dumb to our machines, and I was trying to keep everyone working together in perfect harmony while funding it on my credit cards.

We were starting to ship much larger quantities to distribution centers all over the country, which added a new layer of complexity. Our philosophy was: Get the "yes," and we will figure it out on the backend. Getting the "yes" is the hardest part for most people. Without the first yes, you don't need to waste your time on all the other operational planning and strategy details. Brian started getting very good at getting to "yes" and our production team was not keeping pace with our growth. The only thing we could do was work harder with longer hours, which meant the shifts needed to be longer than they normally were, with fewer breaks and more formality. What started off as part time, cash at the end of each day, with multiple "left-handed cigarette" breaks kind of jobs, was turning into real manufacturing jobs. Some guys liked the money and the thought of working, but others did not.

Each month we were rolling out a new region of the natural foods chain, which required a ramp-up in production, a demo rollout of the region, and then establishing a new baseline of expectations. We were "growing through people," and it was survival of the fittest. It was a very intense time and no small task. To accomplish all our goals, we had to simultaneously scale production, launch the demo and marketing teams, fund it, and keep all our customers happy. Everyone had a job, and we tried to make it as fun and competitive as we could.

For a new regional rollout to be successful, we would divide the region of the natural foods chain into drivable areas. We would then assign a leader to that area who would do demos for two weeks. If the stores were close enough to one another, they could do a morning demo in one store and then drive to another store and do an afternoon demo. The main problem with this plan was the expense of travel. We had no money. We could pay about fifty dollars a night for a hotel and twenty dollars a day for food. This put people in very precarious situations. We always tried to drive, regardless of distance, because you could sleep in your car if you needed to. As we became more efficient with this level of frugality: We figured out that all the hotel apps dropped their price at nine p.m. So, everyone would just hang out until nine p.m., and then see what hotels we could afford. Sometimes the car was a better option because the hotels that switch their price to fifty or under are as disgusting as you are imagining. To circumvent the gross factor, Brian invented what he called the "Diggy Wrap"(spun from his nickname—Digz.) The Diggy Wrap was a sheet that he would lay on top of the bed. He would get into it fully clothed, bring the sheet up over his head to his eyebrows and then tuck the sheet behind his ears. The next step was pulling the bottom part of the sheet up to his chest and over his arm area, leaving one arm available to tuck the sheet under his armpits and ass to create a human burrito. We gave all the sales and demo guys a tutorial on the Diggy Wrap in case they were ever faced with a disgusting motel room, and they all were.

Everyone thinks that expanding your business into a national brand is sexy. Being on the open road, closing deals, changing the world—but in actuality, it's very disgusting and lonely. We never let on that we didn't like it. Positive energy is contagious, and it was our job to spread it. Positive energy mixed with competition is a recipe for success, so we made everything a competition. We would take pictures of the hotel rooms and have a weekly contest for the Most

Disgusting Hotel Room Stay. In our weekly newsletter, we would announce the winner and celebrate their dedication to building the next great American salad dressing brand. It became a badge of honor for toughness and positivity to win the weekly Disgusting Hotel Room Award. Some guys started sleeping in their cars to save the fifty dollars and would take a picture of a dumpster as their hotel room to jokingly try and win.

That positive energy and outlook created a flywheel effect of forward momentum. We were building a brand from nothing, and that was much better than working in a cubicle, regardless of the disgusting hotel rooms. The demos were also positive reinforcement for the team because everyone who tried the product bought the product. Everyone who heard the story wanted to hear more. Even the lowest part-time jobs at Tessemae's were having a huge impact on the growth of the brand, which gave everyone a rare sense of purpose. When we finally started rolling out the California regions, we really felt like momentum was on our side. It was one "yes" after another, and we felt like we couldn't be stopped.

## We Got Stopped

It happened when we hit the NorCal region.

I called Brian to see when the date of the rollout was assuming that region was on board like all the others. But it wasn't. "They don't want us, man," Brian said. "I've been calling, and they won't call me back. I'm not sure what else we can do."

We decided to pull rank and call our buddy, who was the Global EVP of operations at the national foods chain. He made some calls, and said he could get us a meeting with the NorCal buying team, but the regional decisions were still theirs to make.

Brian flew out with his game face on. He called me in the morning to have our ritual Pre-Game Chat, where we reminded each other of everything we had put on the line to get to that point, our goals, our dreams, that we were built for the moment, and of course . . . that we were on a mission from God! I then waited for his post-meeting call. *Ring, ring.* It was Brian. "It's done! Super easy. They loved it. We roll out in a month. I'm not sure what the problem was, but they asked me to stay out here for a couple more days to give them all the details on the launch plan."

"YESSSS! This is huge, man! Excellent work," I said. "Phew, we needed that volume. Let me know if there is anything you need from me while you are out there."

Two days later Brian flew back to Maryland. We met at the coffee shop. And he told me the real story.

"Dude, you're not going to believe this. So, NorCal said no and for me to basically go fuck myself. It was not good at all. As I was leaving the building, I thought: Fuck that. I'm staying here until they say yes. So, I sat in the lobby the rest of the day and tried to get to the guy as he left. He walked right by me and told me to fuck off. You know I ain't goin' out like that, so I went the next morning and sat in the lobby until he got there. When he walked in, I pleaded my case. *Listen, man, I told my brother we got in. He thinks I'm out here mapping out our launch plan. This is my mom's dressing, We have my dad's house on the line. I will buy every bottle back if it doesn't sell, but I am not leaving unless you let me into your region.* The buyer was shocked. He said, "Holy shit, man. I just thought you were another sales guy bullshitting me. If you care about salad dressing this much, I will give you guys a chance."

Brian was smiling from ear to ear as he was telling the story, hoping that his outrageous energy surrounding the story would somehow eliminate the realization of how razor-thin the tightrope we were walking on actually was. I smiled and laughed and told him, "Next time, just tell me what's going down for real, so we can plan accordingly."

NorCal ended up being a very important region for us, not just because of the natural foods chain but because of who else is out there. Another big grocery retailer was headquartered in that area and was planning on selling the retail chain in the coming year. To reinvigorate their brand, they were changing the way customers viewed their product offering by focusing on "special and unique" products and brands. In short, that meant they were copying what the natural foods chain was doing and making those products mainstream. Shortly after the NorCal rollout, we got a call from the produce buyer at the Cal-Chain asking if we wanted to be a national brand for them.

"Nah. We're good," I said.

The buyer paused and said, "Excuse me? We have 1600 stores. You would be in 1600 more stores."

I explained that we were rolling out to all the natural foods chain locations in the country, and that was our focus. The buyer was shocked and told me that he would stay in touch as we grew. And grow we did, by the end of 2013, we had all the regions of the natural foods chain fully operational with a Tessemae's demo person standing in each one. We did so many demos that the natural foods chain changed their demo guidelines to try to prevent us from demoing so much. Before Tessemae's, anyone could walk in and do a demo for a product in their stores. After four years of our demoing like addicts looking for a fix, the natural foods chain changed their rules to "salaried employees of the company only." It didn't slow us down one bit; we just took the average hours of the people working and gave them that salary. It cost a little bit more in taxes, but our mission was to grow, and get the message to the people, not allow bullshit red tape to slow us down.

## The Centralized Solution

Right about that same time, there were whispers that the natural foods chain was going to switch to a centralized buying model and move the power away from the regional decision-makers. That sounded good to us because working with eleven regions of a store chain is like wrangling cats. The global team called to have a meeting at their headquarters to discuss having "a more uniformed and efficient relationship with us." Brian and I flew down, and they pitched us on being in all the stores if we gave them a discount for the increased volume. I pushed back. "We are already in all your stores," I replied.

The buyer looked confused. "How? You don't go through us. So how are you in all of our stores?"

Brian and I explained that we went region by region and sold each team on the Tessemae's brand. The buyer was floored. "I don't think that has ever happened before," he said. "I don't think anyone has become a national vendor by winning over every regional decision maker, that is insane."

"Well, we did it. So, if you want to streamline our order management process by going through one person, we are all in. But you don't have any more stores for us to get into for us to give you a discount."

We liked the idea of having one buyer instead of eleven, and so we agreed to a national rollout with consistent and uniformed shelf space in every store. It sounded awesome in theory but it ran in complete contradiction to our previous experiences with the natural foods chain. Hey, maybe grocery chains can change. But Brian and I knew it was a long shot. And then one day, we received a PO from the global buyer, just like the global team said it would, and it appeared to be exactly what we agreed to. We were shocked. It was amazing. We were doing it! People can change!

Now that the volume was so high and consistent, we could start making one flavor a day instead of four. We could also make inventory for the first time instead of making it "to order" and then shipping it, the second it was bottled, which meant we could manufacture more efficiently with less chaos. Everything started to take shape and come to life like we were a real manufacturing company. We felt like Pinocchio when he turns into a real boy.

We needed to make sure that everything was going to make it to the shelves just as we agreed, so we paid a company to do national shelf checks. Getting a PO is one thing but making sure the distribution centers and stores pull it properly according to the "planogram" is a whole different beast. As the information was coming back on the consistency of the store's shelves, we noticed something peculiar: nothing was changing. Our agreed-upon uniformed shelf space was not happening. It was the same checkerboard shelf space as before.

We called the distributor that we were forced into using and they confirmed what we were worried about: Their warehouses were full of our products, which meant the natural foods chain stores were not. The stores and produce distribution centers were not ordering it from our distributor because the regions were not acknowledging the new process of a "centralized buyer." It felt like the regions were intentionally ignoring the new global team's initiatives.

We called the global buyer in a panic, and he told us the new system was fucked. Everything we agreed to was up in flames. "We fucked up, man. This global buying thing isn't working. The regions aren't listening. The stores aren't listening. The new system isn't being used. It's fucked. I'm really sorry."

There was a long pause, and I asked, "So, what are we going to do? The distributor is calling us and asking what the hell is going on because they are sitting on a nation's worth of salad dressing. We are going to have to buy that shit back unless you get these stores to pull it into their stores. And you haven't paid us because the fucking stores haven't ordered it. We are fucked, not you." He said he felt bad, but his feelings weren't going to help the situation.

My natural reaction to bad shit is to take immediate and aggressive action. I started to think about how we could pull the product from the distributor into the stores; how we could do a nationally coordinated demo program with "super demos" to three times the amount of dressing sold in four hours. I was trying to work this out in my head, And then . . . the phone rang. "You guys ready to be in 1600 stores?" It was the Cal-Chain.

Not only were we ready, we were pretty close to desperate. Talk about the universe conspiring in your favor! I enthusiastically responded, "We sure are! When do you want to get this thing rolling?" The Cal-Chain buyer was delighted to hear that we were ready to partner together and, with equal enthusiasm, told us, "Whenever you guys can support a national rollout is when we will get this going." I responded, "Well, that's right now, so let's map this out!"

We worked with the produce team to map out a national demo program for the Cal-Chain across their best stores. By the end of the discussion, the volume needed to launch our campaign required one million dollars worth of salad dressing. Are you fucking kidding me?! ONE MILLION DOLLARS of salad dressing for one account. We had to play it cool because I am sure Cal-Chain sends million-dollar purchase orders all the time, but for us, it was fucking mind-blowing. It almost didn't feel real. But it was, and for the Cal-Chain, it wasn't even a big deal. They sent over the POs for all their distribution centers like it was nothing, and Brian walked into my office with the POs printed out in a stack. He started to "make it rain" with the POs like he was a pro athlete at a strip club after getting his first paycheck.

After we were done dancing like strippers to the POs falling from the sky like 100-dollar bills, we got to work. We calculated that it was going to take us three weeks straight, working seven days a week with two shifts a day, to make that much dressing. We would have to run both hand-bottling lines and the automated bottling line all at the same time to hit the hourly production goal to ship on time. Which also meant we had to bring on more people.

Despite what you hear in the media about there not being good jobs available for good pay, we couldn't find quality people to work on such short notice, so we hired a temp agency. The only positive part of the temp worker was that we could fire them immediately if they were a bad fit. You just call the temp agency and swap them out immediately. And there were a lot of swap outs. In this high-volume exchange of manufacturing talent, we learned firsthand that most people, regardless of color, stick to their own "group" and don't like "outsiders." So, we focused on our crew from high school to determine who stayed and who went. The Annapolis crew found people who they could get along with and that worked hard. But there was animosity growing between Frank and Darren.

## Culture Clash

Darren wasn't used to this level of leadership responsibility. He was responsible for about thirty-five guys and their output. Frank would ask him to help with maintenance or point out that the machines needed a better cleaning, and Darren took it as an insult. I guess it makes sense in retrospect. I come from a place and time when you got your ass beat if you accidentally stepped on someone's new Jordan's, so a public request in front of your crew to "do better" probably didn't sit well with Darren. We didn't know it, but Darren was starting to self-sabotage.

One day, Darren didn't show up for work or call to let us know where he was. When we finally got in touch with him, he said he was sick and apologized. We thought nothing of it. Then it happened again. And again. This was not good. This was him turning down his lacrosse scholarship in high school all over again. Brian confronted him about what was going on but Darren denied it all. Then one day, he just stopped coming. And remember, at this time, he was living in Brian's townhouse and driving my mom's suburban.

Brian drove over to the townhouse to talk to him, but he wouldn't open the door. This was not good. We gave Darren an ultimatum of coming back to work, and we forget that it ever happened or officially quit and move back to Annapolis. Instead, he decided to tell us to go fuck ourselves, stay in the townhouse, continue to use my mom's suburban, and not come to work.

Did we have a squatter on our hands? We didn't hear from him for about a week, and then we got a call from his wife that the upstairs bathroom was flooding through the ceiling, and she needed my dad's help immediately. My dad drove up to Towson to check on the situation, and the house was completely trashed. Not only was the bathroom flooding everywhere but the entire house looked like someone emptied a dumpster in every room. It ended up being about $20,000 worth of damage. He asked Darren's wife to please pack up and leave, but he received the same message that Darren gave us: "Y'all can go fuck yourselves. We ain't leaving."

My dad was distraught to say the least. "I just can't believe this is happening. After everything I have done for him and his family over the years for them to treat us this way. I just can't." My dad could not wrap his head around what was going on. It took two months to get Darren out of the townhouse in Towson, and we didn't talk to him for a couple of years after that. It was a sad day for Brian but mostly for my dad. He had always hoped that his theory on people and opportunity was correct, and he had a blatant case study showing the complete opposite. The good news is he has never given up on his theory on people and still believes it to this day. I did give up on his theory, though. I was fucking livid, and I started to understand what was required to survive in the manufacturing world of Baltimore. But there was no time to bitch about it, Darren chose his path, and we needed to stay focused on ours.

## Making the Million

The Cal-Chain order was on track to be completed if we kept our insane schedule up of working twenty-hour days. We supplied around-the-clock coffee, food, and very upbeat music so people would stay engaged and focused for as long as they could. But as we entered the last two days, we were behind schedule due to the Darren distraction and it appeared we weren't going to make it. We calculated what needed to be done to finish all the product in time, and we calculated that it all came down to the trucks' arrival times. We figured that if we just made the dressing orders by the specific truck schedule, and kept it out on the warehouse floor instead of moving it into the refrigerators, then the trucks could pull up and get the appearance that everything was done. Then we could slow roll the actual loading process to make up for anytime we needed from a production perspective.

Brian and I took over the hand-filler lines to increase the number of bottles made per hour. We created two teams which we drafted like it was recess in elementary school and put a prize for the winner. Whatever team made the most dressing in one day, received $1,000 and the most important prize of all "Ultimate Shit Talking Rights." That was about $125 a person, but it wasn't about the money, it was about the excitement and pride of competition.

All the guys were facing each other, talking shit the entire day. Brian and I were stoking the fire to get everyone extra amped up. We had a whiteboard that kept track of the completed cases in real time. When a case was completed, someone from your team would walk up and mark it on the whiteboard, look at the other team, talk some shit, laugh, and keep rolling. It was the most productive day of handmade salad dressing production in history. The fun distracted everyone from the fact that we were still going to be cutting it close. Trucks were coming Friday morning, which meant we needed to have the first couple of truck's orders done by Thursday night. But we were behind schedule. We started praying to the "delay" gods about the early trucks being late. We ended production on Friday morning at around two a.m., went home and showered, slept for a couple of hours, and then ramped it back up by six a.m.

The first truck was scheduled to come at ten a.m., which gave us plenty of time to finish the morning orders. At eight a.m., two hours ahead of the scheduled pickup, a truck arrived trying to get a jump-start on his day. So much for the "delay" gods. We knew we didn't have to get it to him right when he pulled in, but our hope of ten a.m. or later was gone. Brian and I jumped back on the hand-bottling line to increase the speed of the production as Matt started slowly loading the pallets onto the trucks as we finished making the rest of the product for that order. This became the rhythm for the rest of the day. By the afternoon, there was a line of trucks down the street. We were literally making dressing, putting it on pallets, and loading it onto the trucks in real time. The production pace didn't slow down until every case was done. We even had a clock guy who was basically making sure we kept a fast pace, so we could get everything done on time and calling out the "bottles per minute" pace we were making so we knew if we were on track.

By nine p.m., we finished our last case. It was done. One million dollars worth of salad dressing made. We set the order out for the last truck on the warehouse floor, and Matt volunteered to wait there and load the truck since Brian and I had been hand-bottling all day. We were exhausted; we were delirious; we had made one million dollars worth of salad dressing.

The next morning, we arrived around eight a.m. to find Matt sleeping in his underwear on a giant sack of shipping peanuts. We pushed his shoulder to wake him up, he popped up and asked "Is the truck here? Did I miss the truck?" We looked around and the dressing was still on the warehouse floor ready to be picked up. "We didn't see a truck outside. And why are you in your underwear?"

Matt was sweating and delirious. "I was waiting for the truck to come and I laid down on this bag of shipping peanuts, the plastic was making me sweat so I took off my clothes. Now I'm drenched in a mixture of sweat and olive oil, and I can't move my neck."

We laughed and told him to get his shit together. He walked over to the giant cleaning sink in the warehouse, where we rinse out fifty-five-gallon drums and mops, got naked, and showered himself off with a hose and some hand soap. Thankfully, no one was there, but you can tell we aren't great with HR compliance. He toweled himself off with paper towels, got dressed, chugged some coffee, did some push-ups, and was as good as new.

The last truck ended up arriving at ten a.m., and we loaded up the last order like we were professionals. It was a fucking miracle. A complete shit show miracle. We pulled it off . . . but barely. We were not prepared for that much volume at once and needed to rethink how we were going to scale the business.

## Field Guide: Lessons Learned

### What You Need to Know
Behavior is consistent.

### How to Do It
This is a two-part explanation: First, People don't change their normal operating processes unless something is up. Secondly, no matter how badly you want the horse to drink the water that you just led it to, the horse chooses, not you. To ground yourself in someone's behavior, you get actual data to create a baseline understanding. We had everyone take multiple different types of personality tests and tools like the PRF test, the CVI, the Myers Briggs, the Predictive Index, etc. That made understanding someone at a deeper level much easier. If someone started to deviate out of their normal behavioral patterns, it was very noticeable. It is a major red flag, and you need to take notice.

### What You Need to Know
Prepare for it all to work . . . even if it's a long shot.

### How to Do It
Our problem was we were being too realistic. "If we pitch them on a million-dollar PO, they will give us $300,000." And when we got the million-dollar PO, we scrambled to make it happen. Ask for exactly what you want and what you can handle.

### What You Need to Know
Radiate the energy you want mirrored back.

### How to Do It
As the leader, you must never forget that you are the conductor of the orchestra. Your tempo becomes the orchestra tempo. Energy can be felt and all of it is contagious whether it's good energy or bad energy.

# SEVEN

We were now in TWO RETAILERS! A total of about 2,000 stores!

The initial rollout of the Cal-Chain business was going really well. Our demo people were going to Cal-Chain's best stores, and the demo results were almost as good as the natural foods chain's numbers. It was pretty crazy, actually. No one could believe that premium salad dressing and demos could work in Cal-Chain. Our buyer was over the moon and so were we.

But it wouldn't last.

A couple of months into the rollout, we got a call from our Cal-Chain buyer. They were being acquired by another grocery chain, and everyone from the original company was either getting fired or jumping ship. "I'm out. I'm not sure who the new buyer is going to be, but good luck."

There was a long pause. "Uhhh, well . . . good luck," I said.

We hung up, and Brian and I looked at each other in a worried haze. But, we figured, this shouldn't be a problem. Our numbers were amazing. Why would anyone want to fuck this up? We stayed positive and kept hitting our numbers and executing the plan.

Then, a call was set up with our new buyer, and we knew we needed the relationship to start out on the right foot. We got on the call, being our normal energetic selves, saying the normal niceties that are said when you meet someone for the first time, and then the buyer hit us with: "I don't believe in demos. I think they are a waste of time and energy, and you guys aren't allowed to do them anymore."

Dead silence. We all looked at each other in a complete panic, trying to mouth what to say next. I remember there being a lot of hand gestures and overaccentuated pronunciation movements with our mouths. I broke the silence. "But our entire relationship with you guys is based on this demo model. All the inventory in your warehouses was built off of the demo schedule. What do you mean we can't do demos?"

No explanation. Just a repeated phrase: "No more demos."

We hung up the phone. Fuck! There was no way we were going to be able to sell through that much dressing without demos. We were going to be fucked.

And we were. For the next two months, our numbers were horrible. We were a new brand in a new retailer that had never sold premium dressings before, and we were basically dying a slow death on the shelf. Things were not looking good. The biggest concern we had was having them call and ask us to buy our dressing back from the warehouse. Our contract didn't say we had to do that, but when that conversation comes up, the relationship is decided right then and there. We were calculating our sell-through rate daily and taking it off of the inventory they had in order to calculate how much dressing we would theoretically have to buy back. What was once the greatest day ever—receiving a million dollars-worth of POs—was now looking like the end of our business if that call came in.

And then . . . we received an email from Cal-Chain. I opened it with trepidation: *Oh fuck . . . this is it . . . the end of Tessemae's . . .* But the email outlined that our demo-hating buyer quit. "YESSSSSSS! There is a god!" And the new buyer coming in used to work with our original buyer and LOVED demos. We were saved!

We reconstituted the original demo plan and started selling the shit out of dressing again. We were so relieved to have a new buyer who was in alignment with our plan. Everything was going well, we were selling through all the inventory, and feeling like the brand was growing again. Then we received another email . . . our buyer quit. Welp, this is not good.

We got on a call again with the fourth new buyer—and guess what? He hated demos. Just fucking great. We tried showing the fourth new buyer the data on demos versus no demos and how much we sold when we did demos. But the fourth buyer didn't care. We were back to dying a slow death on the shelf.

This was now pissing me the fuck off. We needed to get away from whatever the hell was going on and find a retailer that didn't flip-flop on us all the time. As we were mapping out a plan to not get kicked out of Cal-Chain but shift our relationship to one of their large competitors, we received an email: our fourth new buyer quit.

By this point, we didn't know which way was up or down, and we explained the chaotic nature of our relationship to the fifth new buyer. She explained why there was so much turmoil and that she was planning on being with Cal-Chain for the long haul. And to prove her point, she committed to the original demo plan and placed a giant PO for us to get back on track. It was a wonderful gesture and a huge sigh of relief, but the whiplash we were feeling was real. We needed to stop being a Ping-Pong ball bouncing between the natural foods chain and Cal-Chain. We needed to continue to diversify our retailer base.

Brian was on a full-scale mission to get us into a new retailer and was able to lock in a regional test in the mid-Atlantic region with a big box company. They wanted us to do a road show to see if their consumers liked our products and wanted to buy them on a regular basis. It was a six-week process, and they were going to test our top three flavors. The winner of the road show test would potentially be sold in a large custom bottle exclusively in their mid-Atlantic stores.

Well, that sounded awesome. But this big box chain managed their business much differently than other retailers and had a minimum daily volume requirement of $300 per store. That was a lot of dressing for every store in the mid-Atlantic, so we needed to ramp up our sales tactics. Our idea to hit the minimum targets was to create SUPER DEMOS: three demo tables, one for each flavor, a delicious recipe to try for each product to get people interested, nine people to create an insane energy in the store, and recipe brochures that were basically mini cookbooks to hand out.

The road show was amazing. Every single store we were in exceeded the daily minimum volume goals and really made us feel like our brand could go mainstream. Our creative director, Moe, who was our friend from middle school before we hired him at Tessemae's, would stand in the middle of the aisle repeating the line: "Don't cheat yo self, treat yo self—Tessemae's." Brian would walk up to people with a server's platter like he was a waiter and hand them samples. When people would say they didn't want a sample Brian would say: "Yes, you do. It's our mom's dressing, you'll love it." And he'd basically force them to try it. We would bring our children to the demo to play the "cute kids" card to sell more bottles. If they would have let us bring in puppies, we would have done that as well. One big guy came up and was buying chocolate eclairs in bulk and then bought three bottles of salad dressing. If you can win that guy over, you can win anyone over.

But we needed more momentum. Winning on a store-by-store basis was really cool, but how do you win in places where you aren't forcing people to try it against their will? How could we get more people to hear about our journey?

## The Publicity Machine

That's when we made the decision to hire a PR firm. Maybe if people read about how cool our story was and how good the dressing was, they would get interested and just walk into a store and buy our product, no demos needed. Maybe the magazines and TV shows could do the work for us. A bunch of big business magazines picked up our story pretty quickly, and the next thing we knew, we were in *Inc. Magazine, Fortune, Fast Company,* and *Forbes*. Some of the articles were positive and uplifting, a true "American dream" story to pull on people's heartstrings. But some tried to make us out to be ignorant "lax bros" who stumbled into the salad dressing business like drunk frat boys trying to find their beds in the middle of the night. *Fast Company* read, "Can three lax bros actually take the salad dressing world by storm?" Genevieve wasn't happy about the article but if it sold more dressing, I didn't care.

Regardless, we were happy to get recognized and were trying to leverage PR any way we could. *Inc. Magazine* had the largest positive impact. They selected us as one of their 35 Under 35 Coolest Entrepreneurs. We were shocked. As a young guy interested in business, I had a subscription to *Inc. Magazine,* and the 35 Under 35 was the coolest list you could be on—period. We assumed these lists were signs that you had "made it" so we were very excited to be "chosen" to this select group of elite business minds out of thin air. Out of the list of 35, there was the almighty Entrepreneur of the Year Award, which the public voted for. To vote, you had to go on *Inc.*'s website, select what company you wanted to win, vote, and then paste the link on your Facebook page while tagging *Inc. Magazine*. We had a very loyal fan base that was young and very interactive with us on social media, so we thought we had a chance.

In this contest, you could vote as many times as you wanted. There were twenty-four hours to vote and then they would announce the winner. The voting window opened, and we blasted it to everyone we knew: Facebook, newsletters, Twitter, individual emails to large organizations that had been a part of our journey, you name it they received a request to vote for us. Another interesting twist: the results were updated in real time on *Inc.*'s website, so we could see who was winning and by how much. Initially, we were doing pretty well and in the top three. All the companies were steadily increasing in votes at a pretty consistent rate throughout the day but by the early evening, we began to fall behind. We were battling it out for the #2 spot, and as I watched the #1 company began to pull away, I was struck with pride. Here we were, a bunch of salad tossers, being ranked among the top young businesses in the country. Pretty wild.

But then something struck me about the company holding on to the #1 spot. How in the hell was a vegan mayo company getting so many people to vote for them? I'd had their stuff, and it wasn't that good. I got that they were a Silicon Valley company, and so they were considered cool. But this seemed out of whack.

I called a guy who worked for us—Raymond, who ran all of our social media—to see if he thought anything looked suspicious. He used to do some serious hacking back in his college days, and he knew his way around a digital project. And at first glance, he didn't see anything amiss. "Greg, the vegans are loyal. The company is out of San Francisco, and they probably just rallied all the vegan techies to vote nonstop. I'll keep an eye on it and let you know."

Fair enough.

When I woke up the next morning, there was no way we were going to win. We were in second place with four hours to go, and the difference in votes was exponential. But then Raymond called me around ten a.m.—T minus two hours until the contest's voting window closed. "After you called, I started thinking: No one cares about vegan mayonnaise at that magnitude, not even the vegans. And their rate of consistent voting didn't add up, so I went to some of my old hacker forums I used to be a part of and started asking around about how someone could get the voting process replicated on a mass scale quickly."

Raymond soon learned of a service in India that offers just this particular vote-replicating service. So, Raymond visited the forum of that firm and posted the question: Did anyone from our vegan mayo rival make contact with you guys recently?

Then, because Raymond loves a good drama, he dropped his voice like he was telling me a state secret: "Check your text messages," he intoned.

I did. And there in my text message was a screenshot of a conversation between the super cool vegan mayo's head of marketing and the India-based company. It read: "Need about 100 people to create Facebook profiles and post this *Inc. Magazine* link for the next ten hours. Will pay to do it. You get paid, we win, the world is a better place."

I read it again. I wasn't dreaming. These fucking assholes paid a sweatshop in India to vote for them?!

I told him to send the screenshot to the woman running point on the contest at *Inc. Magazine*. It was all we could do. We had a big demo that day so I switched my focus from an elaborate mayo vs salad dressing conspiracy theory over to hustling sauce. The demo went great per usual and as I was leaving the building at around two p.m., my phone started to blow up. *You have 68 unread messages. You have 8 voicemails.* What in the fuck was going on?

I was just about to call Genevieve to make sure everyone was still alive, when my phone rang. It was Raymond. "We fucking did it! We are *Inc. Magazine*'s Entrepreneurs of the Year! Holy shit!"

Stunned, I told him to stop screaming and explain to me what he was talking about. Raymond outlined how he sent the screenshot to the editor over email—and Twitter and Facebook. She started asking questions, and he pointed her to the service so she could see for herself. After seeing the evidence firsthand, the editor disqualified our vegan mayo rival and declared us the winner. I was stunned. I was standing in a parking lot covered in salad dressing, and we were the Entrepreneurs of the Year? Is this what the Entrepreneur of the Year looks like? I thought successful entrepreneurs flew on private jets, and went to fancy parties. They didn't hand out samples every weekend. I can sure as hell tell you that back in college, I never imagined that handing out samples was the epitome of being an entrepreneur.

I called Genevieve, and she was over the moon. "You did it, Greg! You built something that's special. I am so proud of you!" I cut her off, "WE... we... we did it." I'm not very good at accepting praise or telling people, "I did this." I could never be an American politician. But that award, even though relatively meaningless in the scheme of things, was validating for a lot of people at Tessemae's. It provided them with a huge accomplishment that they could point to and be proud of. It allowed them to show the haters that we were gaining traction and making progress. But what did it actually mean in terms of actual substance? Were we special now? Was there a special club where we learn a secret handshake? Did we get to sell more dressing and become rich?

## Nope

We called our PR firm to see how they could leverage the awards to create larger moments for the brand. It turns out: awards don't move the needle much. The only momentum we received from the awards were the moments we created ourselves. Brian started emailing grocery store buyers with the subject line: "Entrepreneurs of the Year that make salad dressing?" It actually got people to open the email and respond, but the answers were the same as before. Nothing immediately came from it like we had hoped. We were let down and a little shocked that this thing we used to covet was nothing more than a visual ego festival.

But then we got a call from a national grocery chain. "They must have seen the magazine!" I told Brian. The buyer who reached out was now responsible for their "new" natural foods department, which was right in our wheelhouse. When we got on the phone, we asked him if he had seen us in *Inc. Magazine*.

"Ummm, no, I didn't. I remembered you and the demos you all used to do in the natural foods chain stores."

We won a national magazine contest. But still, demos were our best sales lever.

The call went well, and he invited us out to their headquarters to meet his team and tell our story, which was a big deal for us. This grocery chain was huge at the time, which meant this was the biggest meeting of our salad dressing lives. We flew to their HQ, and were ready to wow the shit out of them. We had presentations printed in case the projector messed up. We had samples ready for everyone to try. We had hats to give them as gifts. We were fucking ready.

But it turned out they just wanted to meet some crazy brothers and hear our story. They weren't actually interested in us being in their 2,400 stores and just wanted to get an understanding of what was working at the natural foods chain, so they could try to replicate some of that success in their new natural foods department. We left the meeting feeling a little used and frustrated. But we weren't goin' out like that. Brian found the email address of the CEO and sent him the same email subject line he had been sending to buyers: "Entrepreneurs of the Year that make salad dressing?" And then wrote the following:

I know that running a business is tough. Having employees who believe in your values and represent your brand is something we worry about every day. If I had a story like ours (see link), and I could have this brand in my grocery store knowing it was going to sell more product, I wouldn't want anyone passing up on that. Let me know if we can talk.

Sincerely Brian Vetter, Middle Brother

One hour later, the CEO emailed back with his cell phone number and told Brian to call him.

The next day we had a conference call with their C-suite to pitch our brand. The following week we were back at their HQ, meeting with the head of produce. We didn't prepare like we did for the first meeting. There were no hats or samples of dressing. They put us in a tiny room, almost like a closet, and we waited. In any meeting I go into, I think through how I will have to fight my way out if shit hits the fan. It's part of our mercenary mindset. I liked that we were in a small room. I felt in control of my battlefield. And I was ready to do battle to get the "yes."

Just as I prepared myself for combat, in walked a 300-pound man drinking a super Big Gulp. I tried to process this. It didn't feel like a sign the meeting would go well. Brian and I looked at each other with "Oh fuck . . . this isn't good" expressions. The buyer sat down and pulled out some charts on lettuce trends. "Thank you for coming in, guys. Take a look at these charts: Romaine lettuce is trending down, and tender leaf greens are trending up, like baby spinach and mixed greens. Ranch is too heavy for tender leaf greens. That's why we need a lighter dressing for those lettuces. Your dressing would be perfect for those lettuces. Can you produce for all 2,400 stores?"

Shocked, we nodded our heads, and said, "Yes."

"Excellent, I will send you the paperwork, and we will roll out in January for the New Year's resolutions crowd. Thank you for coming in."

We stood up, shook his hand, said nothing, turned, and walked out. The meeting literally took two minutes. When we got outside, I looked at Brian in complete shock. "Did we just get in 2,400 stores?" Brian replied, "We just fucking doubled in size?!" We hugged and screamed, "WE ARE DOING IT!" We took a selfie in front of the company sign and sent it to everyone with the great news. People were shocked. How in the hell was the little-ass salad dressing brand getting into these giant retailers?

## Our Hollywood Moment

Buzz was starting to build around our story and our journey. One day I received a call from a Vancouver, British Columbia, phone number. It was from a guy named Zach, who said he was an MTV producer. "Greg, my buddies and I have started a production company and want to make a reality show with you and your brothers. I read about you in *Inc. Magazine*'s 35 Under 35 and was super blown away."

A little taken aback, I asked him to explain what this would entail. Zach wanted to film a teaser, which is a longer version of a trailer, and then pitch TV networks. They would need us to let them film our lives for about two weeks, and then they could boil down what they needed from there. While he was speaking, a million different scenarios went through my head, most of them not positive. Did I really want to be dealing with this type of bullshit right now?"

I told Zach I would talk to the family and circle back.

When I put it to the family for discussion, only Brian was excited about the idea. I was on the fence because we needed to start selling more dressing, and the plan we currently had was very labor intensive and required an unbelievable amount of backend support to execute. We needed more information to make such a big decision so Brian went to one of our food brokers to get any data on TV shows and their effect on CPG sales. The broker came back and showed us the top three products in Walmart at that time were all *Duck Dynasty* items. The show about the colorful Louisiana family business was on fire, and every product they launched in retail was absolutely killing it.

Thinking about the positive impact we could have on the salad dressing brand started getting my brain moving. Genevieve wanted nothing to do with it. My parents were indifferent. Matt couldn't have cared less, Brian wanted to do it, and I was trying to figure out a way to sell more dressing. I tossed it around in my head, weighing all the reasons we should or shouldn't do it. We came to the conclusion that we would do the teaser and then see what network wanted to pick it up. Depending on the network, we would make the final call at that time.

I called Zach back and said we all needed to meet and discuss the structure of the relationship, so we flew out to LA to meet the team. When we arrived, the producer was supposed to meet us at our hotel, but he texted us that he had a "spur-of-the-moment break dancing lesson" at the gymnastics facility nearby.

We told him we would meet him there to learn a couple of things ourselves. He was shocked. "Are you guys fucking with me? You want to learn break dancing moves?"

We were not fucking with him. I said, "We are from public school. The more dance moves we know, the better. Also, we have been sitting on a plane for seven hours. What better way to get things moving."

Half of me wanted to get loose from the trip, and the other half wanted to see what the fuck happened at a spur-of-the-moment break dancing lesson.

Turns out, a spur-of-the-moment break dancing class was a common thing in LA. There were about thirty people in the class who randomly showed up at the drop of a dime. The class was legit. Brian, Matt, and I went through all the exercises and drills with him and laughed the entire time. The instructor may still be scarred from our fearless attempts on the trampoline. We learned the proper form for a front flip and then a backflip, and then the three of us started having a competition to see who could do the most backflips to front flips in a row with perfect form. The instructor was not prepared for three meatheads to be competing during his spur-of-the-moment break dancing lesson. The producer thought it was hilarious. "I cannot believe you guys came to the break dancing lesson and then were dominating flips like that. That was insane. You guys are fucking wild."

We laughed and walked back to the hotel, where Zach gave us a brief rundown on the agenda for the trip: Dinner at his house with the full producer team, meet at their office the following day to outline what the show would look like, dinner with their business partner the following night, informal meetings at studios the following day, and then party that night.

It seemed a tad aggressive, but we were ready to rock. LA's lovely climate masks the chaotic shit show of its highways. When I asked, "How far away is it in miles?" they all looked at me and chuckled. "Bro, LA traffic is so crazy it could take you an hour to go a mile, so you don't talk in distance. You talk in time."

Sounded super relaxing, I thought. To live here, you have to love traffic.

The producer crew pitched us on their vision for the show and it sounded pretty good. We conveyed our concerns about our family name and legacy, our children and protecting them, and making the brand grow in a positive way, not as a joke. They all agreed that was the plan, and we went out to meet with some studios to, in their local lingo, "talk about the idea of the idea." Everyone seemed overly interested but in a potentially fake LA way, but we were still feeling pretty good about it. Everyone we met said the same thing: "Feeling like this is the next *Duck Dynasty*."

It made me think: did we want to be the next *Duck Dynasty*? I was hoping for more of a *Hard Knocks* on HBO or *All or Nothing* on Amazon vibe. The producer crew said the meetings went better than they expected, and they needed to bring in some bigger guns, so they looped in a big name—Scooter Braun. Scooter Braun is the talent manager who discovered Justin Bieber on YouTube and convinced his mother to take him to every radio station in the country to turn him into a star. It obviously worked, and Scooter became his manager. In addition to Justin Bieber, Scooter represented Kanye West, Demi Lovato, and Ariana Grande, to name a few. This dude did not fuck around and was about my age. He also played a college sport—his was basketball—and we had a lot to chat about. He thought it was hilarious that three former lacrosse players were making salad dressing and thought our energy was perfect for a national TV show.

As the night progressed, he invited one of his new clients to dinner to hang with us, and it turned out to be Psy, who had the hit K-pop song, "Gangnam Style." This was hilarious because his song was currently #1 in the world and had broken the Internet, and here we were, betting this dude he couldn't chug beer faster than us. In our informal competition, we won every time, and he blacked himself out. The next thing we know, he is dancing around the restaurant doing his famous Gangnam Style dance. What a wild world where a bunch of salad-dressing-making brothers are partying in LA with music moguls.

But LA wasn't our vibe. It's never good when the most common compliment you receive is: "You're so authentic!" I still don't know if that was a compliment or an insult, but it was said often. It reminded me of the soft insult so common in the South: "Well, bless your little heart!" Regardless, the trip came to a conclusion, and we scheduled a time for the crew to come out and film the teaser, while we got back to planning our world domination through retail channels.

## Recipe Reset

Now that we were in the natural foods chain, two traditional grocery chains, and a region of a Big Box chain, we felt like we were crossing the chasm into Real Brand Land. Our company still seemed small to us but we were making significantly more progress than other brands that launched around the same time. Our first grocery chain client was going better than expected and had turned into our #1 retailer, accounting for 50 percent of our monthly revenue. It was amazing to be able to plan more efficiently from a production and inventory perspective. Not only could we plan better but we could monitor data better as well because the grocery chain had just bought the leading retail data company. For the first time, we had access to sales data that drilled all the way down to who the consumer was and what else they were buying. Everything felt like it was going our way. Until we received a call from our grocery chain buyer in October of 2015.

"I have good news and bad news. The good news is Tessemae's is the most loyally bought salad dressing in all our stores. The bad news is, it's the worst-performing dressing for new customer shelf sales. We think this is because it's not certified organic and it is solidified on the shelf."

And then he lowered the hammer: If we did not fix both these issues by January—the company's annual "reset" period—the chain would drop us.

Panic hit my gut, and my hands started to sweat. We had been in their stores for about eight full months and built a dedicated team just to support them. They had their own account rep, support person to the account rep, sales broker, and all the additional manufacturing people we needed to bring on to support their volume, AND NOW we were about to lose them? What they were asking was no small feat. The organic certification was the easy part of the Herculean lift they were requesting, and even that wasn't easy. What we needed to do in addition to that was almost impossible. We needed to change the recipe to all our dressings, find a new oil, get the product certified organic and certify the facility, design new labels with the organic certification, get them printed, and get all of that back on the shelf before we got kicked out in January.

Here's something about the consumer packaged goods industry that consumers may not know: Reformulating a product isn't just changing the recipe. You need to start with food science, get process authority sign-off, conduct shelf-life studies, procure the raw materials in large enough volumes to support a national retailer, potentially rethink how we make it all because it's a new formula, and then communicate the changes to all the retailers without having to change our UPC codes, (which would require resubmitting all the paperwork for every product as if we were a brand-new company).

We rented a conference room in Baltimore to sit down and figure out how we were going to do all of this. The first couple hours were spent thinking about miracles that could occur that allowed us to pull this off without much effort. The rest of the day was spent mapping out the insane amount of work ahead of us with deadlines that were nearly impossible to make. Regardless, we had our marching orders, and we were going to need a fucking miracle to pull it all off.

The biggest issue was the oil selection. What oil was similar in taste and health profile to our existing recipe but didn't solidify in the refrigerator? We had hired Kristen as our head chef and head of product about a year earlier. She was the one who needed to reformulate all the dressings with the help of my brother Matt. But she had not been with us in the early days. She had not gone through the Tessemae's Obstacle Hurdling Olympics with us. And she needed to get her head out of Corporate America, where everyone debates what could go wrong, and join us in the mindset that this was: Tessemae's—the land where miracles happen every day. I worked with her on this. "Stop being formal," I told her. "Just start every call and email with: I really need your help. My life is basically on the line, and I will do anything to make this happen."

She looked a little puzzled, but I promised the phrase would cut through all the bullshit and at least give us a chance of accomplishing the miracles we needed.

Matt started ordering certified organic versions of our oil from all over the world with rush shipping. Our FedEx bill was not cheap. Oil samples started coming in, and we immediately started our tasting process. Kristen would do blind taste tests with a sheet of paper that had all the little cups listed by number. We would try the oil, write down our thoughts, retry the oil, confirm our thoughts, and rank our top three in order of why. She would look through to see if there were any similarities in ranking, which there usually were and then narrow it down to the top two.

Kristen and I usually had similar tastes. Matt was very close to ours, and my mom always had interesting insights. Brian made up answers and was usually wrong. And Genevieve's were the opposite of mine.

After taking mini shots of oil for thirty minutes, we narrowed it down to Expeller Pressed Sunflower Oil. The oil couldn't solidify in the refrigerator, which eliminated the options of olive, avocado, and coconut. The other oils we tried were too pungent or random in flavor and didn't taste well as dressing. We were concerned some oils were just a fad like grapeseed oil. But sunflower oil seemed like people would understand what it was, appreciate the health benefits, appreciate that it didn't solidify in the fridge, love the taste, and buy more of it.

A week into this process, we had selected a new oil, reformulated our most palette-sensitive product, and sent it off for food science and shelf-life studies. Once that information came back, we could redesign the labels, send the art to the printers, notify the retailers of the changes, and keep the process rolling. Our most important task: Lock in the organic certification. There are multiple groups that handle USDA organic certification, and Kristen began reaching out as soon as we were close to new formulas. They came back with a timeline: six months. That's how long they said it would take to certify our products and the facility.

Kristen began to panic. "None of this means anything if we don't get it certified organic! This will be a giant waste of time! We don't have enough time!"

Kristen is one of the most magnificent people I have ever known, but her creative process takes a little getting used to. She turns bright red and points her pointer finger up on the side of her face as she presses into her cheek like she is punching herself. When she reaches her boiling point, she starts telling you about how it won't work. When no one listens to her, she starts cussing you out. When everyone tells her to calm down so we can help her see how it CAN work, she flicks everyone off and storms out of the room, often leaving for the day leaving everyone concerned that she might quit. And then, come the next morning, she will be in the test kitchen, listening to 90's gangster rap with the "impossible problem" already solved.

The organic certification process followed this pattern: Kristen called three of the four agencies that could do it, and they all told her to fuck off. Kristen told me my advice was worthless. "I did your stupid little fucking saying, Greg, and no one gives a fuck!"

I laughed and told her to call the fourth one, and then, if it didn't work, I would call them all myself. She called the fourth certification group, and a surfer bro from California picked up. He said, "That's crazyyyy, chef. Yours is my favorite dressing. I was just telling a dude who works next to me how lit this would be if we got to do the organic cert on your all's stuff, cuz I knew you guys were going to do it eventually, and here you are. This is so lit. I will definitely get this done for you in no time."

Kristen was legitimately in shock. My office was right next to the test kitchen, and I heard the entire conversation. I walked next door, smiling. "Don't even smile at me, Greg, that was just fucking lucky," said Kristen. But I kept smiling. "Put yourself in situations where serendipitous shit can happen, and it usually will," I told her. She looked at me with her squinted death eyes. But had a hint of joy. "He was super nice, and I am very happy, now let's move on," she said.

A major win in the Herculean effort category. And now we could finalize the art for the labels, notify the retailers, and keep chugging along.

The reason for the January deadline was the volume of dressing purchased by consumers for the "New Year, New You" season. Everyone sets New Year's resolutions to get healthy, and they buy the fuck out of our dressings. January, February, and March pop the fuck off for our brand. The category review for dressings for big grocery chains was in March, which meant that if we didn't get on the shelf with the new products that were organic and didn't solidify, we would miss out on some of the volume of January and go into the category review with nothing to show for it. We were on a mission and had to get the product made and on the shelves.

The element that demanded the longest lead time was the labels. They had a six-week lead time, and we were trying to get the printer to do it in four. That would put production right in the beginning of December, so we could get everything out the door for January. As the days ticked by, everything was falling into place, and we were just waiting on the labels. Raw materials were showing up like clockwork, bottles arrived, and we were pushing hard on the labels. We were going to pull this off! At the 3.5-week mark of lead time, Matt called the label guy and was told they were on track to have the labels done by the four-week mark.

But they weren't.

The label guy called a couple of days later, and said they ran out of the paper we normally use, which comes from overseas, and there was nothing they could do. I tried another tactic. "What if we change this round of labels to something else? What else do you have in the building that could work?" The printer called and said we could switch to a thinner plastic label that had the potential to crinkle more when being applied to the bottle—but they had it in stock. They could start printing the next day, and we would have to pick it up from their plant in New Jersey with our own truck.

We rented the good old Penske truck with a lift gate again, and Matt set off up the New Jersey Turnpike as a truck driver. Driving a thirty-foot box truck for four hours on the highways sucks, just in case you haven't done it. Doing a round trip in one day *really* sucks. Matt pulled into our plant at seven p.m. with the labels on board, and we began making dressing through the night. As we made pallet after pallet of dressing, a feeling of accomplishment and relief came over me. A major obstacle to consumers buying our dressing was finally solved. We listened to the retailer and made it happen. And bam, we were becoming a real brand. We called the grocery chain buyer to find out when they were going to place POs for all the new product that were being made so we could order the trucks.

The buyer said, "Whenever we sell through the old stuff."

Silence . . . .

"Excuse me? We just reformulated all our products and certified them organic for the January reset like you asked us to. What do you mean after we sell through the old stuff?"

The buyer responded that they weren't going to eat the cost of the old product to put the new stuff on the shelves.

We hung up the phone and started brainstorming. "What if we bought it all back?" I asked.

Brian didn't love the idea. We'd just spent a lot of money to reformulate everything to organic.

But if we didn't do something, we were going to get kicked out of the chain in March when our numbers looked bad.

Brian decided to call the buyer and see if we could split the cost.

"No."

Brian went back and asked if we could pay for it over time.

"No."

Brian went back again and asked if we could ship the new product, swap out the old product, and then not charge the grocery chain for the new inventory. So, it would be just like buying back the old stuff.

That got a yes.

We had a secret plan to make this work without going broke. Our plan was to ship enough new product to get it on the shelves, then space out the POs, so the buyer would see how well it was selling and maybe not make us buy back all the old stuff.

We kept that goal to ourselves.

We started shipping the new product to the grocery chain at the beginning of December. It had taken us thirty-seven days to reformulate all the products, get them certified organic and the facility, get the food science done, and then begin production. Thirty-seven days, that's it. We knew how big that was from a productivity perspective but none of that mattered if consumers didn't like it more than the old product.

As the product hit the shelves and January rolled around, we waited to see our fate. When would we know if this new product was going to sell better? Would there be a backlash around the sunflower oil? Did anyone care about organic? Was this the dumbest thing we had ever done? January 1 came and went, then the 2nd and the 3rd, no word on sales data. January 4th, 5th, and 6th came and went, still no word. I began to panic. Does no one fucking care?! Did we just go out of business? I started to get really worried. Brian had been reaching out to the buyer with no communication back, which made everything seem so much worse.

And then, on January 8th, we received a frantic call from the buyer: "This week has been absolutely insane! I forgot to reach out to you guys, but can you rush order me twice the amount of dressing you normally send? It's sold out. I will email you a PO later today, but I need you to get working on it right now."

There was silence in the room. We looked at each other. We looked up to the sky. I put my right hand on my heart: Thank you, God.

## Field Guide: Lessons Learned

### What You Need to Know
Listen to your customer before it's too late.

### How to Do It
The customer isn't always right. But when you hear one thing enough times, they may be on to something. Track all your customer service emails and put them in categorical buckets. Look for common themes in complaints or positive notes. Combine all that information with your gut vision of where the product and brand should go.

### What You Need to Know
Anything is possible if you are crazy enough to believe it.

### How to Do It
When you are trying to solve a problem or accomplish a goal, ask questions. Be a stubborn asshole with peoples' answers. Break everything down to its simplest, most fundamental form, and then ask more questions. More often than not, people just try to complicate things because they are lazy and don't want to do extra work. Keep pushing until you get what you want.

### What You Need to Know
Put your blinders on and focus.

### How to Do It
Take pride in being obsessed and focused on your goals. Ask yourself questions in the morning to get your mind right: Does this help me reach my goal? We never should have distracted ourselves with the thought of a TV show. We were hoping the TV show was a silver bullet . . . there is no silver bullet. There is only the journey, and the journey takes one solid step after another . . . there are no shortcuts.

# EIGHT

The reformulation and organic certification changed everything.

Non-congealing salad dressing really does sell better than salad dressing that looks like it's frozen. Who knew?

By May, we were cranking and getting the data to make better decisions. I had an itch to change our packaging. Other brands were starting to replicate our bright colors, and we needed an evolutionary change.

## Betting the Ranch

We reached out to some marketing agencies and began the process. At that same time, we decided to gather more in-depth data, to supplement what they gave us for free. We found out "ranch" dressings were 68 percent of the salad dressing market—because consumers were using it for everything from chicken wings to crudité. Meanwhile, our dressings that were considered "fruit forward/vinaigrettes" were only 18 percent of the market. We had ten dressings living in the 18 percent segment. What that meant was we needed a ranch dressing, or we would never grow.

We had an R&D meeting to discuss how we could make a clean ranch dressing that didn't use dairy or thickening agents, was organic, and tasted great. Kristen hit us with the beginning of her creative process—the part where she gets very red and tells us off. "Ohhh, those are the *only* parameters I need to work within? No dairy, tastes great, no thickening agents for a dressing that is as thick as glue!"

She stormed out.

And like clockwork, the next morning, I walked into the plant, and she was the first one in the test kitchen, bumping 90's gangster rap. I poked my head in to say good morning and saw her smiling. "Greg, I think I got it!" She figured out we could use egg yolk to thicken it. Since we were the leaders of this clean food movement, we couldn't use any legumes or powders with weird additives, and her creative capabilities were handcuffed by the paleo, Whole30, and clean-eating mobs. But none of that stopped her.

She kept grinding, and two weeks later, she called me into her kitchen. "Try this!" she ordered, shoving a carrot in my mouth drenched in ranch. It was fabulous—I mean next-level delicious.

She went on to walk me through how the egg actually added a lot of amazing flavor to the ranch. If we could figure out how to make it on a mass scale, then this was our recipe.

We called Matt in and explained what needed to be done. Matt and Kristen immediately started working on scaling up the recipe to see if we could make it in mass quantities. This was going to be big. The first-ever "clean, organic, great-tasting ranch, that was dairy-free" are you fucking kidding me!

While the ranch phenomenon was taking place, we were making big moves on the packaging. Our marketing lead, Charles, worked with the marketing agency daily to lock in the packaging evolution of Tessemae's. I came up with the theme: Going from high school to college. You're still the same person, but you are very different . . . almost a little sophisticated.

(OK, that wasn't my experience in college but it was a good instructive theme to give the marketing group.)

All of this started coming together. We were creating ranch dressing and delicious variations of ranch, like avocado ranch, that could compete for more customers. We had our organic certification, non-solidifying dressing on the shelves, and potentially new packaging. We were going to take over the world! That's how it felt, at least. As the packaging began to take shape, it was fucking beautiful. We narrowed it down to three themes, and then I took the three home. I have a good design eye and came back with a combination of all three and gave it to the agency. They did their thing with our CMO's guidance, and what came back was magnificent. This was going to be big. We decided to do a massive launch at the Produce Marketing Association (PMA) Fresh Summit in Orlando at the end of October.

## Creating a Legend

The PMA Summit is the largest produce show in the world, with countries setting up booths to show the produce they grow and export. To put how big this show is in perspective, the previous year, my brothers and I couldn't afford a booth, so we were walking the show trying to find retail buyers. We would go to all the big booths like Church Brothers, Taylor Farms, Driscoll's berries, etc., and we ended up partying with the execs of a major fruit company. This big fat guy who enjoyed his cocktails and partying loved our energy and walked us into all the VIP parties at the show. As we were shooting the shit, we were talking about how well a meeting went with the grocery chain buyer, he patted me on the head and said, "I just met with fucking CHINA. CHINA MOTHERFUCKERS. They want my citrus! I don't know if I'm going to give it to them, but they want it!"

Brian and I looked at each other in disbelief. We were out here selling to a grocery store chain, and this dude is selling to a fucking country.

And so, with that story in mind, we knew we had to launch all of our innovation at the PMA Summit. We reached out to the president of the PMA Fresh Summit to see if we could still get a booth in a relatively good area since it was so close to the actual event. Brian had worked hard the previous two years to meet the produce elites when we were trying to sell our dressings to salad suppliers. At a previous PMA meeting in California, he signed up for the Tour De Fresh, which is a 350-mile bike race to meet the ballers of the growing world, and showed up in normal workout clothes. The pro bikers looked at his ass in disbelief. "Where is your cycling kit? Is that what you are planning on wearing?" Brian had no idea how serious the race was and told the lead bike mechanic this was his first time on a road-style racing bike. The mechanic, in complete shock, told him: "Give me your fucking credit card. We are going to buy you everything you need so you don't die."

Brian biked that event, and the Legend of Brian Vetter and the PMA Summit was born. So, when we called to get a booth, we got it. As the packaging was unfolding and the PMA Summit was locked in, we wanted to create a gigantic splash. We knew the ranch would be a winner, but we wanted to go bigger. We called one company to see if they wanted to reinvigorate an idea we had the previous year, which was single-serving salads in retail. They were open to the idea the previous year but we just didn't have the tools in place to make it really work. Now they said they would give us some space in one of their buildings to hand build the salads.

Innovation time: We designed five salads and, in the process, decided to take one of the components of the salad and make it its own retail item. Salad toppers were born. Think seeds, crunchy things, dried fruit, and sometimes bacon in a little pack that you dump on the lettuce to give it depth. Brian started calling retailers to give them a little sneak peek of what was brewing, and a grocery chain came back and said they wanted to have a meeting about all our innovations the day before the show.

Say what?! We already had a meeting? This was getting bigger and bigger by the minute. Now we needed a theme to get people to the booth. Because we signed up late, we were not on the main strip, but we WERE within walking distance without too much of a detour. In true rebellious-joy fashion, we decided to tweak the biggest name in ranch. We made the theme of our launch: "There is nothing hidden in our ranch."

Then we splashed our theme all over everything we had. We designed the logo to look just like the Hidden Valley logo, made tee shirts, and made the entire side of our booth a billboard saying just that. People were talking! And Hidden Valley would surely try to sue us! We couldn't buy better publicity. The packaging was fucking beautiful. The products we were developing were fucking beautiful. Things were working like they had never worked before.

As the event grew closer, everyone started to get excited. We had never done a food show before. We created a ranch dressing that would change ranch dressing forever; we had an innovation list longer than a CVS receipt, and additional produce innovation items that had never been created. The energy was electric. Looking back on it, that was our moment. It's the moment every brand dreams of: Retailer interest beyond our capacity to even execute. That was the dream, and hitting it was an amazing feeling.

All eyes were focused on the national grocery chain preview. This first tour would determine the rest of the show because they were seeing everything before everyone else. If they loved it, we could go into the show with complete flow and confidence. If they hated it and word got around that everything we had created was shit, the show was going to be horrible.

We arrived three days ahead of time to set up the booth, make all the samples, reserve the hotel suites for the meeting, and make everything as perfect as it could be. Only Brian and Chef Kristen would be at the preview and the rest of us would be waiting to see how things panned out. We all helped prep the products in the hotel suite for the meeting and then went back to our respective hotel rooms and tried to distract ourselves until we got word on how it went. I went to the gym to work out some anxiety while nervously checking my phone every forty-five seconds. One hour went by, and nothing. And then an hour and a half. Still nothing. I left the gym and started walking to my room and the phone rang. "They want it all. They loved every single item we showed them, and they want it all!"

In total, that was twenty-six new products. We currently had four dressings with them, and they wanted all twenty-six. I was in shock. I ran over to the suite where Brian and Kristen were and everyone had already sprinted over as well. We started hugging each other and jumping up and down. It was fucking amazing! Complete shock and pandemonium ensued. The risks that we had taken up to that point were validated in that moment. We were going to make it. We were going to be the next great American brand. Holy fucking shit.

We all celebrated that night and went to dinner to take it all in. People were the happiest I had ever seen them. It was the greatest thing that could have ever happened as we entered the PMA Summit to unveil the new packaging and innovation. We had the largest food retailer in the world signed on for everything we made.

The show kicked off the next day, and it was pandemonium. Every retailer in the country was at our booth to see all of our innovations. Word had spread, and people wanted to see what all the hype was about. We could do no wrong. For three days, we met with retailers about growing the brand in their stores, negotiating exclusivity arrangements around certain products, mapping out joint marketing campaigns, and everything in between. We left the show knowing everything had worked. All our work in packaging design, new product creation, and messaging had been a home run.

All that was left was a final meeting to lock in the specifics with the grocery chain.

## The Rumble and the Stumble

Our buyer was a big football fan, so Brian got field passes for the Bills-Bengals game and made a day of it. Our CMO, Charles, our Tessemae's grocery chain account rep, Brian, and our buyer spent the day at the football game and then went out to dinner afterward to keep the energy flowing. At dinner, after a full day of drinking, everyone was chatting about how big and fast the football players were from the field level. Brian talking his normal shit, said that he could have played in the NFL if he had chosen to do so. Charles then started busting his chops, saying Brian sucked at sports, and the routine competitive shit talking began. Both Charles and Brian played college lacrosse, so their competitive fire is alive and well. The only difference was Brian played professionally and had me as his older brother beating his ass from an early age. Charles started saying that he could beat Brian in any sport on the planet, so Brian accepted the challenge and told him to choose something. To add some spice to the bet and the shit talking, Brian bet Charles that if they were to wrestle, Brian would put him on his back in less than one second. Charles accepted the challenge.

They went up to Brian's suite to keep the party rolling with smiles and laughs about the upcoming challenge. Our account rep took out his phone to film and announced the wrestling match like it was a main event at Caesar's Palace. They both approached each other, and Brian faked high, put both hands around Charles's waist, and folded him to the ground in less than one second.

There is film of Charles' face. There was contempt there. Even rage. This wasn't just a wrestling match; this was something more that no one knew about. Charles was broken.

My phone started blowing up. It was two a.m., so it took awhile for me to pick up. Charles was yelling and slurring his words, and all I could decipher was: "I'm fuckin done. Fuck all of you." And he hung up. Brian had been calling me the entire time as well, and I called him back. "Charles's a fucking asshole . . . he challenged me, and now, he's crying about it like a little baby."

I told him to sleep off his liquor and to get his fucking mind right because we had the biggest meeting of our fucking lives at 11:30 a.m.

At eight a.m. Charles called again and was sitting at the airport. He had quit and was flying home. I said nothing. I called Brian. "Charles fucking quit, Brian. Did the buyer follow you up to the suite?! Does he know what the fuck just went down?"

Brian paused to reflect through his drunken haze. "No, he didn't come. He doesn't know what happened."

"Go get some coffee, go to the fucking gym, sweat this shit out, and lock in this fucking meeting," I told him.

He did just that. He called at 12:30 p.m., and the deal was done. He made up something about Charles having a family emergency so the buyer didn't get distracted and never mentioned his name again. The biggest deal in Tessemae's history was complete . . . and we almost fucked it up.

I couldn't help but think of the fourth obstacle in "Accomplishing Your Personal Legend," written by Paulo Coelho in his 10th-anniversary edition of *The Alchemist* "Then comes the fourth obstacle: the fear of realizing the dream for which we fought all our lives."

Coelho referenced a famous Oscar Wilde quote: "For each man kills the thing he loves."

"And it's true," Coelho wrote. "The mere possibility of getting what we want fills the soul of the ordinary person with guilt. We look around at all those who have failed to get what they want and feel that we do not deserve to get what we want either. We forget about all the obstacles we overcame, all the suffering we endured, all the things we had to give up in order to get this far. I have known a lot of people who, when their personal calling was within their grasp, went on to commit a series of stupid mistakes and never reached their goal—when it was only a step away."

Coelho also wrote, "This is the most dangerous of the obstacles because it has a kind of saintly aura about it: renouncing joy and conquest. But if you believe yourself worthy of the thing you fought so hard to get, then you become an instrument of God, you help the Soul of the World, and you understand why you are here."

Renouncing joy and conquest. That's what Charles did. He was right there. Everything we had fought for, every struggle, every obstacle that was overcome, and the prize was right at his fingertips. And he couldn't move forward. But that was his decision, not mine.

We focused on the gigantic win and what needed to be done to execute it. We were going to focus on launching the new dressings first in January for the "New Year, New You" season. The grocery chain wanted a ninety-day exclusivity for the new packaging and to roll out all the new products first, which we happily gave them. January hit, and all hell broke loose. Ranch dressing, avocado ranch dressing, and habanero ranch dressing, combined with the new packaging of existing products on the shelf, increased our shelf sales by 300 percent. It was like drinking from a fire hose. It was everything we had ever dreamt of times ten.

But now we needed to figure out how to maintain that level of volume from a manufacturing perspective without screwing everything up.

## Field Guide: Lessons Learned

### What You Need to Know
Be prepared to win beyond your wildest dreams.

### How to Do It
Have a theoretical plan that you will implement when the dominos begin to fall. Too often, we plan for some "realistic" scenario of success instead of something much greater. In thinking too small, we don't actually prepare for the big win to happen. Prepare for greatness. Envision three different scenarios that are beyond your wildest expectations and think through what will be required if they happen.

### What You Need to Know
Create things that you are proud of.

### How to Do It
Be a motherfucker about the quality. Don't cut corners. Don't make excuses. Don't settle for mediocrity. The reason we got the yes for twenty-six SKUs in the world's largest retailer is that we made products that were amazing and didn't cut corners.

### What You Need to Know
Check in with yourself during the journey.

### How to Do It
In manufacturing, we call it "preventative maintenance." How can you stay at, or as close, to 100 percent as possible? There are little things you can do daily, weekly, and monthly to make sure you are grounded and focused. One of the things I do at least once a quarter is read the 10th-anniversary introduction to *The Alchemist* to make sure I'm not committing any of the four obstacles of Achieving Your Personal Legend. There are also little things I do daily, like journaling, reading, meditating, ice baths, etc. Everyone will have their own "preventative maintenance" plan.

# NINE

The minute I arrived home from the PMA Summit, I knew we had to raise money to match this new growth. The magnitude of the opportunity we were sitting on was too important to keep on the road we were on. Brands wait their whole lives and never get this moment. I wasn't going to let this slip by.

## Money Quest, Take One

I started reaching out to investment bankers about raising twenty million to support the growth we needed to take advantage of this moment. We needed a quick turnaround, and we needed the deal done by no later than February—which was four months away.

Most bankers wouldn't talk to us. We were too small. They had never heard of us. Our timeline was too tight. While I was trying to get a banker to take us on, one of our early seed money investors, Tom, suggested an option: Tom knew a guy who he said was very effective in this space. Tom had invested with him when he was raising money for another brand. He thought this would be a good fit for Tessemae's.

I trusted Tom and still do, to this day. He built a tech company from nothing and sold it in his early forties and is just a great guy.

So, I decided to explore this option. We met his group for lunch in Columbia, MD. Tom's guy, Jerry, walked in. There was something about Jerry's blue eyes that said: trust me. Jerry was a graduate of a U.S. military academy and had served in the Marines. Now, he ran a business that offered financial advising, planning, and money-raising assistance for smaller brands.

By the end of our lunch, Jerry Blue Eyes was all in. "This will be done by Christmas, and I'm so confident in my abilities, I'll put $250,000 of my own money in this deal to prove it to you." Well, that was putting your money where your mouth was. So, I said: Fuck it. Let's go with this dude.

We started getting all the materials together, and in the first two weeks of Jerry's work, we had 1.5 million dollars in the door. *This guy can really make moves,* I thought.

And then I received an email from Jerry's partner. "I have left the company and taken the staff with me to start a new firm. When Jerry fucks this up, let me know, and we'll take over."

Excuse me?!

I called Jerry Blue Eyes. "Everything cool, man?" He explained it wasn't a big deal and all of his clients who were going to invest in Tessemae's were already locked in. This was just a business partner being greedy. My Spidey Sense was up, and I knew this was not good. But if the money was coming in the door, then I was good to go. We needed to be closing about two million a week to be done in time for the grocery chain launch.

But after the first 1.5 million, the money stopped.

Around Thanksgiving, I called Jerry, and he acknowledged that he couldn't do it anymore. His partner's defection freaked everyone out. He was too distracted trying to save his own business to raise the rest of the funds for ours.

I was livid. "What the fuck are you talking about, Jerry! The grocery chain launch is still fucking happening, and the support plan we promised them requires a large investment from our side to pull it off." He apologized and hung up. I sat in disbelief for about five minutes and thought through how I could keep everything on track.

Fuck!

## Money Quest, Take Two

I got back on the phone and started calling people. No one, and I mean NO ONE wanted to take this Herculean feat on. Then I was referred to a guy who had just started the investment banking arm of a big bank. He was starving for deals and would do anything. He said he would fly down that Monday to meet with us. Excellent! But I needed one more option in case this guy didn't pan out because time was running out. Someone had referred me to a guy out of Chicago who specialized in growth businesses. He said he could fly in the next day, which was Friday. Even better!

We set up the conference room to put our best foot forward, brought in lunch, put on polo shirts, and were ready to impress this guy. The banker needed to sell us, but in reality, we needed to sell them. We needed a "true believer" who was completely dedicated, so they could pull off the money in record time.

The Chicago guy walked in looking worn down. He could've been forty or sixty for all I knew. His skin looked like it hadn't seen natural light in years and glistened from stress—almost like he was covered in Vaseline. We sat down, and he began to sell me like a whiny first grader. "I don't know how anyone is going to get this done," he said. "This business is kind of a piece of shit. No wonder the first guy fucked it up. You really need to be an expert in these types of shitty deals to be able to navigate the chaos."

My blood started boiling. After about five minutes straight of this fucking nonsense, I looked at the guy and told him, "I want you to pack up your shit and get out of this building." He looked at me. "Are you kidding me? I just flew here from Chicago to help you raise money." I stood up. "You have three minutes to get out of the building before I beat you within an inch of your life."

After he scurried out, we all sat in the conference room, disappointed and let down. "This dude on Monday better not be a piece of shit like that asshole," Brian said.

Monday came, and the bank team arrived. The polar opposite of Vaseline Boy walked in with a team. Kyle played D1 football, was a go-getter, knew our brand, and wanted to make a name for himself with his new office. He said raising the money by February was a stretch, but he would do everything he could to make it happen. We signed with Quarterback Kyle that day and were off to the races. We immediately went on road shows to San Francisco, New York, and then Boston, with five-plus meetings a day, selling people on the vision for Tessemae's future. All that had really happened was a commitment from the grocery chain on all the new SKUs and new beautiful packaging that wasn't yet on the shelf. And this proved to be an issue. People wanted to see what would happen when the packaging hit the shelf. Now, a kindergartner could have looked at the old packaging and the new packaging and predicted the new packaging was going to crush it. But kindergartners are more creative people than people in fuh-*NANCE*. That's how all those arrogant assholes say finance: "I'm in fuh-*NANCE*." At first, I didn't even know what they were saying.

All the unnecessary bullshit surrounding the money raising was a complete waste of time, but that was the game. We started gaining a lot of interest and had about fourteen groups to consider. Then it came down to us selecting who could potentially be a good partner. Time was an interesting component of the raise because people wanted to see what would happen with the packaging launch. Then when the packaging launch happened and completely crushed it, they wanted to see if the growth was going to be sustainable. You really can't win with these types of assholes. The goalposts are constantly moving, and the more precarious the situation becomes for you, the more leverage the finance guys get from a negotiating perspective.

As time went on, our results were getting better and better so the focus switched to a new demand: Could we deliver from a capacity perspective with all the new growth? By the middle of January, we had narrowed it down to four groups, and the targeted close date was now pushing into March. We went on another last-minute road show in Boston, but that's where things started to unravel.

## The Snowflake Snafu

We had brought on a finance chief. She was a world team college athlete, a Top Ten MBA, and former president of a family business that sold for a big-ticket amount. But she was having trouble dealing with the stress we were all under. As we were walking to a meeting in Boston, it began to snow. BIG snowflakes fell from the sky. It was actually really beautiful. But as we entered the lobby at our meeting's location, she took her briefcase and softball pitched it into the wall, and screamed, "I HATE GETTING WET!"

The record stopped, and everyone looked at her in shock. I broke the silence with, "Are you fucking cool? What the fuck is up?" She was on the verge of crying. "I hate getting wet. I hate it." "OK, that's fine," I said, "but we have a meeting in five minutes, so why don't you get your shit together."

We entered this entirely mahogany room with old oil paintings on the wall of ships this dude's family probably owned when they conquered America. Our finance chief took out her laptop for the presentation—it was destroyed. The pitch against the wall had detached the screen from the keyboard and there were wires hanging off. The screen itself was cracked. I gave her a nasty look and then turned my attention to our host. "These Boston streets are mean even for laptops! Thank God we aren't Yankees fans!" Everyone laughed, and I proceeded to give the presentation from memory. We salvaged the meeting. But our finance chief's outburst was a major red flag, and I was now super concerned she wasn't going to make it to the finish line of these money deals.

Turns out, I should have done more than worry. About a week later, I was on a money-raising call and my HR person appeared at my desk and said she had a Code Red in her office. I shrugged it off. Our HR leader was young. Maybe she didn't know what a Code Red meant? I walked with her to her office, where my finance chief was nonchalantly sitting on the edge of the couch, casually smiling. I addressed them both. "What's up, team? I need to get back on this money call."

She looked at me, and said, "I gotta run."

"OK, to where?" I asked.

She tried to straighten out her smile. "I mean, I'm leaving right now. I can't handle this stress. We're growing too fast. We don't have the money to do it. We're traveling all over the place. I quit."

I turned bright red. "Are you fucking kidding me? We are at the finish line. We have four groups who want to give us twenty million, and you are going to spook all of them now and fuck it up. What are you doing?"

She said nothing. She just picked up her trashed briefcase and left.

HOLY FUCKING SHIT. This really was a Code Red. By the time I got back to my own office, our now-ex finance chief had already emailed the four groups. She must have done it the second our HR leader came to get me. All of them started calling me, viewing it the same way I did: A big, fat disaster. Two groups immediately backed out. Apparently, your finance chief leaving right before you take on twenty million dollars does not inspire confidence. We were then left with two. One was the home office of a billionaire in Boston, and the other an up-and-coming CPG private equity group with some guys my age operating out of Los Angeles.

## Old Money vs Young Guns

We called both groups, and they didn't seem overly concerned. They said things like: *These things happen. We will make it work.* But I knew things were not good. In addition, time was starting to hurt us. We were growing like a fucking weed, and everyone was fronting us credit because they thought we had twenty million coming in. We were starting to get squeezed by our suppliers in terms of how much they were willing to front before they got paid.

The Boston billionaire home office was in no rush to do a deal. They had all the time in the world. But we didn't. The young up-and-coming LA guys wanted to do a deal because they were young and ambitious. We trusted the home office more but liked the energy of the LA Young Guns. I called them both to see who could close on the deal the fastest, without saying it in those exact words. The LA Young Guns guaranteed we would close in thirty days. That was good because that's all the runway we had left. The home office said they didn't know when they could close, and they were in no rush.

I called our three-person board (which we had created a few years before at the time of our early seed investors) and let them know the responses. We were all in agreement—and we signed with the LA Young Guns.

At first, they promised we'd close and get our money by the middle of March.

The lawyers began redrafting the operating agreement and governance controls for the new partnership. Middle of March came and went. Now they said the middle of April was the new target. As we entered May, we were hanging on by a thread. We had hired an entire office to support all the retailers we had brought on. Manufacturing was running twenty-four hours a day, payroll was massive, and we were constantly scrambling for cash. I called the guys to see what the fucking deal was, and they promised it would be done before June. We let the suppliers know to keep them at ease and focused on closing the deal.

On May 31 at 10:30 p.m., my birthday, I received a call from one of our LA Young Guns.

"Hey, man. We are closing tomorrow. Everything is good to go. Just need to run a couple things by you before close. You need to fire your brothers, fire your CMO, and if the cash balance in your bank account falls under eight million dollars, we take over the board. If the sales metrics are missed in a single quarter, we take over the board. And all hiring decisions will go through us."

Dead silence on the phone. The entire money-raising process ran through my brain. His partner's nasty, smug attitude echoed in my head. Their fake support when the CFO walked out now made sense. This was not good. I managed to choke out, "Let me talk to the board, and I will call you tomorrow."

That night, I couldn't sleep. I was shocked. Was I going to lose everything I had worked for to a bunch of LA pussies who wore V-neck Merino wool sweaters with no undershirts?

I told the board the next day what was going down, and their only response was: "Oh my God, what are we going to do?"

But I was in fight mode. "I would rather go down in a fiery blaze trying to save this thing myself than give it to those fucking pussies," I said. "I'm going to call them and tell them to go fuck off, and then I will have a plan of attack of how we are going to turn this thing around."

My next move was to return the call of the LA Young Gun, who had ambushed me less than twenty-four hours previously. "Hey, man. I talked to the board, and we aren't doing that bullshit. Good luck with everything, but we are out."

He was fucking shocked. "No, no! We'll go back to the old deal!"

I replied, "Nope, we're done. I no longer trust you, and that's that."

He then replied, "You know what, I respect that. That takes balls."

Yeah, fuck you, you LA pussy.

## Money Quest, Take Three

I called Quarterback Kyle, our D1 football investment banker, and told him what had happened and what our decision was. He was concerned. "There's no way anyone is going to give you money now that the CFO walked, and you walked from the deal, regardless of how fucked it was. You have to wait this out. If you can survive through this, there'll be opportunities for you on the other side."

He was right. He tried calling all the other groups who were interested, and they all said there were too many red flags. I spent the month of June trying to find twenty million dollars. It did not happen. On July 7th, we met at one of our conference rooms to map out our turnaround. We basically had to fire everyone, find some sort of short-term financing to pay back our suppliers to keep the product flowing, and then find a longer-term solution to keep the growth going.

It was a tough pill to swallow. To go from lighting the world on fire to staring at an Excel spreadsheet calculating how many of our 120 people we needed to fire to survive is a very soul-wrenching experience. Maybe it's different for giant companies because they don't know the people, but for us, every person we hired was like family. We were about to give terrible news to people we cared about, and it was entirely our fault. Self-inflicted wounds are the worst to deal with and the worst to find solutions around because people can always point the finger and say, "If you had just . . ."

The meeting was intense, and all five stages of grief were in full effect. People were screaming at each other about who to fire and who to save. Asking someone to value their team to decide if they live or die is a fucked-up exercise. But we did it. We had to fire thirty people, and that was only the first phase. We actually needed to fire about fifty total, but I wanted to see if I could pull off a miracle, which meant if we didn't solve our problems, there would be at least twenty more people gone. The message to those we kept was: "Be a Swiss Army Knife." We told them: "If you stay, you will have to do not one job but three jobs. If you don't want to do that, then leave and let us save someone else."

Only three people didn't want to stay.

In addition to reducing people, we also had to "fire" retailers. Most of our retailers approached organic salad dressing like rap music in the early 90s: They just thought it was a fad, so we had to convince them to let us in their store by giving them sweetheart deals. Now, we called the retailers and were very blunt: "You can change your price and the financial arrangement with us so it works for both parties, or we are no longer sending you product." Almost every retailer we called about changing the financial arrangement told us to fuck off. That left us with a group that included the grocery chain, the natural foods chain, a Big Box Retailer, and Tessemaes.com. That was 80 percent of our volume anyway, and they were also the most flexible with our situation. They told us to just keep shipping product and keep them in the loop. We went from fifty-five retailers to four. It allowed us to take a deep dive in to how much infrastructure we actually needed to make the product and support it.

Then came the hole we had been digging and were standing in. It was four million deep, and it would take every ounce of our capabilities to get out of it.

We called all the suppliers and let them know our situation. Most of them agreed to stay with us if we called them every day with an update. But we also needed to start paying off what we owed, which took daily negotiations. "If you ship us a truckload of oil, I will pay you for one and a fourth loads, and I will keep doing that until my debt is paid off." That had to happen every day for every supplier. But not everyone was that understanding.

Our first supplier lawsuit began during that time, and it wasn't even because we owed them money! When you cross the chasm from child to adult, as we were crossing with our company, you are forced to start making very tough, aggressive decisions, and it changes you forever. You no longer play nice or act like a weakling in moments of conflict. The threat of "lawsuit" no longer matters because there is a more dangerous threat looming: The threat of the end.

So, we met our first lawsuit with a shrug. One of our suppliers for salad toppers sent us the finished product with live bugs sealed in the plastic. Live bugs! We took videos and pictures and sent the pictures to the supplier so they could resolve the problem and send us new product. But this guy wanted to be paid for the bug bags. "Pay us, or we file suit!"

We tried to reason with him, and he didn't care. We told him: "Well, then fuck it. If you want people knowing you make products with fucking bugs in it, file the suit."

And he did. Not only did he file the suit, but he also called our local newspaper and made up a bunch of bullshit about us not paying him, and the newspaper wrote a fucking article about it without vetting it!

If our suppliers and investors weren't spooked before, they were now. Not only were we trying to save the brand, trying to make product, trying to do what was right, while trying to keep the lights on, but now we had a PR crisis on our hands. We lawyered up and filed a countersuit. Our lawyers also called the newspaper, and they took the article down but it was too late; the damage had been done.

At the same time, our Instagram account was hacked, and we were served with a price we needed to pay to get it back. Surprise, surprise—it was exactly the same amount of money we owed

Bug Guy. What a coincidence. *Now we don't have social media?! What the fuck?*

Genevieve called one of her friends who worked as a lobbyist for Instagram and had them intervene and unlock our account. We hired a forensic tech ninja to track down the hacker, who, turns out, was from the same area as our Bug Guy, but we couldn't prove it was him.

We refocused our efforts back to money raising. The only sources of capital I could find were "merchant cash advances." It's basically loan shark money. They look at the retailers you have, how much cash is coming in, tap into your checking account to do a daily cash sweep, and will loan you money based on the incoming cash for the month at 35 percent interest. You read that correctly: 35 percent interest. We were now entering Doomsday scenarios. The merchant cash advances allowed us to start paying suppliers for raw materials, but we were just kicking the can of our financial obligations down the road. I needed to find an actual solution. No one would loan us money because of the situation we were in—NO ONE. We tried getting accounts-receivable-based lines of credit, but no one would work with us because of our produce business. When you work in produce, you have to deal with some very specific regulations. There is a law called the Produce Agricultural and Commodities Act (PACA), which helps farmers get paid within thirty days, or they can notify the PACA trust and file a claim. If they file a claim with PACA, the government can just come and take the money from the business account. And if the business account can't cover the bill, PACA can come after officers personally.

Banks do not like PACA. Every road we went down was a dead end, except those merchant cash advances. I just kept taking them to keep everything alive. We were up to about three million dollars in merchant cash advances while continuing to pay for a 1.5 times rate on raw materials. Every dollar we made went out the door, and then some.

It was not good. Things were looking bleak, but I was going to leave no stone unturned.

Then we heard that a company in our orbit had just sold for 1.6 billion dollars—and they had started a family office. We knew the executive team from the PMA Summit and called the former president to see if he wanted to invest in Tessemae's. Since we used to be competitors, and we used to beat his ass in sales. He said yes and flew in to see us.

This was going to be our moment. We got the manufacturing plant spotless and set up an entire presentation of what happened with the money raising, and how we could fix it. When he arrived, we dived in to how we could structure the deal and start working through it. Every detail appeared that we were in control. Questions were flying back and forth, and it looked like this was going to move forward, and we were going to save the day with this new partner. Then—and this is not a joke—the lights shut off.

All the power went out. The conference room went completely dark, and there was a moment of complete silence. I just sat there: *Are you fucking kidding me? Is this really happening right now? Of all the fucking moments to get the fucking power shut off, this is the day it happens. FUCK!*

I looked at our visitor and shrugged my shoulders. "Can't get any worse than this, right?" I half-joked.

I walked to the finance office that had multiple windows for light and asked if we had paid the bill. We had not. I told them to call the power company immediately and pay the fucking bill regardless of how much it was and to get the power on ASAP.

It turned back on thirty minutes later. But in those thirty minutes, all the energy of a "fair deal" that I felt in the conference room was gone. If you are ever in a negotiation with someone about anything, try not to have every weak component of your life exposed in the middle of it. It's really not a great negotiating tactic.

The visitors still wanted to do the deal, but now they basically wanted everything. They asked to go out to dinner with our original seed money investor duo to discuss their proposal. But when they told our investors about taking over the business and doing nothing to keep Tessemae's investors intact, our original backers, who had been with us for years, said no. "I'd rather take the zero and write it off than just hand it to you without the write-off," said one.

The other investor called me after the dinner and let me know there was no deal.

We were so close. An inch away from the finish line, but I didn't think about that. I just replied, "Roger that," and I went back to the drawing board to try to find a way to save Tessemae's.

## Field Guide: Lessons Learned

### What You Need to Know
A sense of urgency and preset deadlines are not good for negotiations.

### How to Do It
Pretend you have all the time in the world. Don't let anyone know you need their help by a certain date. You would think that potential investors would love the fact that you have giant opportunities for growth that are pouring from the heavens. And in one sense they do, but on the other side of that, they know you are too emotionally vested in the success of the opportunity to negotiate well because of the time crunch.

### What You Need to Know
Keep calm and carry on.

### How to Do It
Start reading about Stoicism. For years we had been screaming from the rooftops that "one day we will be big." And when that day came, and investors wanted to know why they should invest with us, my initial inclination was to continue screaming from the rooftops, "Because now we can be bigger." That emotion is not working in your favor. Be almost emotionless. Be methodical. Be a stone-cold killer. The emotion that is boiling in your soul is not working in your money-raising favor. I found the Stoics a little too late and could have used it during these times of important decision-making. *Per aspera ad astra* which translates to *through hardships to the stars*.

### What You Need to Know
Omens are good . . . even if they are bad.

### How to Do It
Have faith and trust your process. Imagine you're watching a movie about your life. What part of the movie did this particular omen pop up in? You may not like the things that are happening to you or the signs you are receiving, but all of it is for a reason. Don't try to convince yourself that the signs you are receiving are somehow good when you know they are bad. I look back now, and everything that happened was for a good reason. At the time, I felt like the world was out to get me. But in reality, the world was trying to steer me down the correct path . . . which was not the one I was on. And that was going to make the movie way more interesting.

# TEN

With each passing day, things got a little more stressful. I had not solved ANY of our money problems and at every turn, things were getting worse. And it wasn't only normal bad news I was facing, it was the possibility of solving all your problems and then those possibilities getting demolished just short of the goal line, over and over again.

That was beating me down. It wasn't the strength needed to overcome the obstacles that was going to kill me; it was hope. Every day was the same cycle: wake up, drive to Essex while attempting to solve problems, think I was going to solve them, get so fucking close I could touch the victory, and then—nothing. Go home, wake up, and repeat. I started to wonder if I could die of a broken heart.

As I was trying to find meaning in my suffering, I thought about Admiral James Stockdale and his experiences, later coined the Stockdale Paradox. I felt like this was exactly what I was dealing with. I kept reading and found a lot of comfort in his perspective. "What is the reality I am facing right now, and how can I manage through it?" was his mantra. I stopped asking myself a million questions that led to endless suffering like: What kind of test am I supposed to pass here? What actions have I taken during the journey to require this level of pressure test? Why was this happening? Was there a deeper message I was missing? An omen I missed? An act I needed to pay penance for? How in the hell did I get myself into this situation?

Instead, I wrote out a quote and kept it in my wallet. Every morning before I started my day's trek through hell, I would read it: "The true measure of a man was not where he stands in moments of comfort and convenience but where he stands in moments of challenge and controversy." Being negative and weak wasn't going to help anyone accomplish anything. I needed to get back to leading by example and refocusing my mornings on preparation—preparing for battle mentally, spiritually, and physically. I had gotten off track with my morning routine by working on the twenty-million-dollar deal with the LA Pussies because of the time zone differences.

I got back to a wake-up time of four a.m., wrote my "morning pages," meditated, prayed, read through my Moleskine to see what the day looked like, planted my tactical seeds for the day based on my critical and important lists, read something impactful like Marcus Aurelius' *Meditations*, and then went to the gym. When I left the gym by seven a.m., I was prepared for anything. I had lived an entire day already, I was prepared to trek through hell or whatever came my way.

That preparation allowed me to attack the day's problems with a greater sense of vigor and "a middle finger up" mentality. I was leaving no stone unturned, and the problems of the day weren't getting any easier, but my approach to solving them had dramatically changed. My morning mantra became: *My focus is on today; I will be present; I will solve today's problems; I will live today like it is my last and go to bed knowing I had done everything in my power to set myself up for tomorrow knowing that I am fully prepared to fight again leaving no stone unturned.*

Everyone around me was losing faith and energy trying to solve these Herculean problems knowing we could fail at the last second. We all knew about banks and their lack of flexibility around PACA. We all knew a new group couldn't get a creditor's first position on anything for collateral. We all knew we were four million in the hole. It was a lot to try to ignore and still stay positive while we pressed on, but we had to. It didn't matter that it was hard, there was no other option.

## Money Quest, Take Four

Then we found a somewhat sketchy accounts receivables-based financing business out of Atlanta, who was willing to allow us to factor our invoices with them. Now, everyone had said this before, and the deal always failed, so I understood where the rest of the team was emotionally, but we didn't have another choice. But this time I decided to only answer questions when I was asked them, and not proactively tell them anything. This method worked and got us farther than we had ever gotten with a financing group. All we had to do was get our actual bank to release a PART of their blanket lien to allow this Georgia-based group to have a first position on AR. That seemed reasonable, so I called the bank and explained the situation.

Our banker listened, asked a couple of questions, and then said no. Not only did they say no, but the call spooked the shit out of them, and now they were worried. They decided to assign a member from their "High Risk Team" to monitor our account over the next couple of months. Are you fucking kidding me! This was an additional layer of bullshit that I did not need, which then added a new layer of anxiety. Was the bank going to call our 1.2 million note?

But we were just too close to the finish line to give up now, and I was forced to go back on a universal principle I have with people: When you break my trust, you are dead to me. I called a guy that I no longer trusted, but he was still connected to us and our success: Mickey, one of the guarantors on our 1.2-million-dollar loan.

Mickey was an early investor in Tessemae's. Our bank had introduced us because he had a law firm with a specialty in entrepreneurial firms. Mickey said that he specialized in the situations faced by high-growth companies and all the legal and financial complexities that come with that. Or at least that's what he told us. We realized later that Mickey was using the law firm as a front to get in with high-growth companies and siphon off their ideas. I won't get into the entire situation here because it probably requires its own book, but the short version is: I had an idea. He tried to steal it. We had to sue.

Mickey was NOT at the top of my list of people I wanted to call. But I had no other option. It was either live to fight another day or die right now. So, I called him. I explained that his name was on the loan with the bank, and if the bank didn't release the first position lien on AR, we were going to be fucked. He asked a couple of questions. His attitude was: Why are you calling me about this?

I reminded him that if we defaulted on the loan, the bank would be knocking on his door for the money.

That got his attention. He suddenly took interest in solving our problem, and said he would make a call to the bank to get more details. The next day he called with some interesting news. The bank was willing to sell Mickey the loan for half of what we owed, thus opening up the first position for AR so we could get the line of credit with the Georgia group. I had never heard of a bank doing that, but it was good news, nonetheless. Mickey then asked, "How much do you need to really grow this thing? I know you were raising twenty million, but did you really need all of that? What was the real number?"

I told him it was about seven million to execute the plan with the grocery chain with full support, which was our highest priority. Mickey called back the next day and said he had a plan. "I will raise the seven million for you if you give me equity and a board seat for doing it. We'll pay off the bank, the rest of the money will go to growth and this will all be over."

I was silent on the other end of the phone. I thought about my complete lack of trust in him versus having no other option. Should I choose to live to fight another day or die now? I told him I would call the board and call him back.

The board all agreed Mickey's plan sounded a little sketchy but it would allow us to survive. I called Mickey back and agreed to the deal in theory and connected him with our lawyers. He started setting up meetings to raise the seven million with a heavy focus on the first 1.2 million dollars to satisfy the bank and get some cash in the door. The original plan was that he was going to buy the bank loan for half, as he'd described to us, and take on that liability and risk. That domino would fall and then allow us to implement the factoring arrangement with the new semi-sketch Georgia bank. That would show everyone our plan had merit, and the rest of the money would follow.

## Enter Jack

The first 1.2 million dollars came in. And it all went to the bank. Mickey didn't buy the loan at all.

The rest of the money was supposed to "fast follow" after the bank was paid off, but Mickey wanted to add another element to the project. He called and said he wanted me to meet a U.S. military academy grad who specialized in money raises and only used the funds from other military grads. It sounded like the most honest thing to ever come out of his mouth. Most academy grads are great people, so I met Jack the Military Guy and Mickey for lunch.

Jack said he could get the deal done in three weeks. He had already made the calls and things were teed up. That sounded very fast to me, but hey, ya never know. Later, Mickey called me and said the money raise would go faster if Jack appeared to be an internal employee doing the raise—with a title of Head of Strategy. I said, "I don't care what you call him as long as he brings in the funds."

We set up Jack as a 1099 contractor, and he started showing up at the manufacturing plant to get a better understanding of the company so he could pitch the deal "more passionately." Jack's passion quest was a complete distraction for the entire company, and the funds did not come in like he promised. A month went by, and aside from the first 1.2 million dollars (that Jack didn't even raise; that was all Mickey), all Jack did was walk around the manufacturing plant, distracting people from doing their actual jobs.

Something was not sitting right. There was an energy in the air that this dude was up to no good, but I couldn't put my finger on it. One day I randomly received an email from our landlord asking how I was doing. I called him.

"What's up, my man?"

My landlord replied, "Hey, is everything alright over there?"

"Yeah, why?"

"I just heard a nasty rumor at the golf club, and I just wanted to make sure you boys were OK."

"I'm sitting in 'beautiful' Essex, Maryland, as we speak."

We exchanged surface-level updates, and he ended the call with: "OK, good, just making sure."

Something was up. Why the fuck would my landlord call me? I'd spoken to him twice in my life! My radar was up, and I was on high alert.

A week later a lobbyist friend texted me the same thing. "You good?"

Why was everybody asking me that?

I called him back. "How come you're asking me if I'm good?"

He said he wasn't exactly "in the know" but he'd heard a rumor that Tessemae's wasn't doing well.

"Could that be because I'm in the middle of a turnaround right now and getting the absolute shit kicked out of me?"

He laughed and said that must be it.

Something was definitely up. There was too much weird energy floating about, and I don't believe in coincidences. I called my lawyer and asked him how the contract review was going with Mickey's team and he said: not good. They kept trying to change the contract. My lawyer would send his comments with edits to their changes, and then they would change everything back and try to slip some new bullshit into the contract. "This thing is never going to get done at this rate. They keep trying to change the deal every time we speak."

What could they be up to? Were Jack and Mickey working together? Was Jack just trying to take my job like any other corporate-climbing whore.

And then my CFO came up to me and said, "Jack just said the weirdest thing to me. He said that he thought I was really smart and wanted to keep me around. What the fuck does that mean?"

I found clarity right in that moment. I answered her, "Jack thinks he is going to take control of this company with this new money raising." My CFO had a lot of questions, but I told her to just be very nice to Jack and to keep giving me information as she got it.

Jack only needed to be there to get money in the door. So, all the other distractions he was causing presented a good pretext to call Mickey—then I could chat him up for more intel.

I called Mickey to see where the rest of the money was. It had been two months, and nothing had progressed. We were paying Jack for his 1099 services with nothing to show for it. I told Mickey that if Jack didn't raise the rest of the money in the next two weeks—he was gone.

As I walked back inside from the parking lot, Jack was standing right there. "Any leads on the funds?" I asked him. He said, "Yes." But he had a weird tone in his voice. I said, "Holy shit, that's great news! Who is it?" I asked. He looked at me and said the names of the LA Young Gun Merino Wool V-Neck-Wearing Pussies.

My blood instantly boiled. "What the fuck are you talking about? We walked from that deal. We aren't taking their fucking money!"

Jack said he couldn't find anyone else—claiming it was the only option he had. All of his contacts turned down the deal and the LA Young Guns had reached out to him to see if we were still interested.

"How in the fuck do they know who you are?" I wanted to know. Jack made up some bullshit that he was known in the private equity world, but I wasn't buying it. All the pieces of the puzzle were there, and now I needed to put it together to be able to take action. I called my lawyer and told him what I thought was going on: these guys were trying to take over my business. My lawyer thought I was making up a conspiracy in my head because of how stressed I was. In my lawyer's defense, I only had the pieces, not the completed puzzle. But the pieces were coming together:

- Mickey lied about buying the loan.
- Jack hadn't raised any money.
- My CFO said Jack said something weird about keeping her around.
- The landlord emailed me to check in.
- My lobbyist friend asked if I was OK.
- The LA Young Guns were back on the scene.
- Not really incontrovertible evidence, but I was convinced.

## The Plot Thickens

The next week, everything reached a boiling point. Jack said he was going to Vegas to meet the LA Young Guns team, but they didn't want me there. I said, "Excuse me? What the fuck are you talking about? We aren't taking their money, so why are you going to Vegas?" He said he didn't have any other options and was going. I called Genevieve to make sure I wasn't overreacting to the moment, and she confirmed that this was a "declaration of war" moment.

I called my buddy Aaron, a consultant who was our outsourced finance department at the time. He had become a trusted resource for me and always brought a very different perspective to situations. His dad and family were all homicide detectives, and he was the only one who ended up becoming an accountant, so his point of view was very unique. He had a good eye for bad guys.

I told him I needed a sanity check with my conspiracy theory and explained what was going on. He told me to meet him at his office at seven that night. We sat in his office going through all the facts and all the situations, and he didn't like any of it. "This is fucked, man. Jack is definitely up to something, but I don't know how Mickey plays into it." I told Aaron how I thought it was all intertwined and that Mickey and Jack were trying to stage a coup with LA Young Guns capital. Aaron laughed and said, "That would be some wild shit. If you are right, fire Jack right now. If Mickey is involved, he will call you in less than one minute. In any crime my dad was trying to solve, the first person to speak was the guilty one."

We called our lawyer. He went over Jack's 1099 contract and told us we didn't need to give him a "heads-up" on termination. I called Jack at around 8:30 p.m. "Jack, effective immediately, you are terminated from your 1099 contract."

And I hung up.

Seventeen seconds later, Mickey called my phone.

I didn't pick up. I looked at Aaron with wide eyes. He looked shocked, and we both said at the same time: "These motherfuckers are working together."

My lawyer was on speaker phone when I made the call to Jack and was still on when Mickey called seventeen seconds later. All my conspiracy theories were true but didn't have substantial evidence to take real action. All we knew was that we needed to get these guys out of our lives, and our current situation was more fucked than we had previously thought.

I called Genevieve and told her what had happened. She was generally sad for me due to the never-ending ass beating I was in the middle of taking, and that wasn't going to be ending anytime soon. I drove the hour home from Aaron's office and called Mickey back as I pulled into my driveway. I wanted to let him stew for a while but acted like nothing was up when I called. "What's up, man? I saw you called."

"Hey, umm, you can't fire Jack."

I heard panic in his voice. I replied without emotion. "Yes, I can, he's a 1099, he's done nothing, and I don't need him."

Mickey then replied with even more panic in his tone, which was not his normal demeanor. "We really need him, and I will pay him out of my own pocket to keep him engaged."

"Why would you do that, Mickey? He hasn't raised a single dollar and the only money he found was the outfit we rejected once before, and we aren't taking their money."

"You just can't fire him!"

I elevated my voice. "Well, I already did, and that's that, so I don't know what to tell you."

Mickey kept trying to invent a reason why Jack needed to stay, and I finally just hung up the phone. I sat in the car thinking about how insane this scenario had become.

And then my phone rang again. It was my CEO coach, Andrew. I'd started working with him three years earlier. He was a Baltimore based CEO and leadership coach that Mickey had introduced me to when we first started working with his law firm.

"What's up, Andrew?"

"Greg, you can't fire Jack."

"Wait . . . *what?!*"

He said it again. "You can't fire Jack, Greg."

This conspiracy theory of mine was apparently underestimating the situation. The forces against me were much, much bigger.

"Andrew? How the fuck do you know what I am doing?"

"Mickey just called . . . there are too many things in motion for you to get rid of Jack. You will be committing suicide."

Andrew was in on it? My fucking advisor? Am I taking fucking crazy pills? I went into full Hulk Rage mode. To this date, I have never screamed so clearly and loudly for so long at anything or anyone in my entire life. I was in my driveway, in my car, with the windows closed, and my wife could hear the entire conversation from inside the house.

"YOU WERE FUCKING IN ON THIS SHIT?! YOU WERE MY FUCKING ADVISOR, MOTHERFUCKER! HOW THE FUCK COULD YOU DO SOMETHING LIKE THIS! DON'T EVER FUCKING SPEAK MY NAME OUT OF YOUR MOUTH AGAIN."

I hung up the phone, with my heart beating in my neck. I was furious but also realized that I was in the middle of some serious shit.

I never spoke to Andrew again.

## More Mickey . . . and a Minor Miracle

Mickey texted me that he wanted to have coffee the next morning at 7:30 a.m. He still didn't fully know what I had pieced together, so I decided to play it super calm and like nothing had happened. Let him think it was all just an emotional young entrepreneur having a rough night.

I walked into the coffee shop, and Mickey was sitting at the back table just like my youngest brother Matt had been years ago when he came back from Denver. Mickey was sipping a latte of some sort with panic all over his face. This dude was up to some shit and in some big trouble.

"What's up, man? How you doing?" I asked. Mickey tried to keep it light, but then jumped right in. "We have to bring Jack back on. You lied to investors. They invested in Jack. You're going to be in some serious trouble. I mean big trouble. These investors are really pissed."

I casually sipped my espresso like a complete sociopath and replied, "No, Mickey, you're in big trouble. I never spoke to those investors. You're in big trouble. You keep saying I'm in trouble. But it's not me, it's you." His face started turning deeper and deeper shades of red while he tried to remain calm with his tone. "I mean we, we're going to be in trouble."

Again, casually sipping my espresso like a mob assassin: "What kind of trouble are WE going to be in?" He started jumbling his words and talking in circles. He got angrier and angrier, talking about financial crimes and misleading investors. Jack had to be brought back, etc., etc. I cut him off. "Jack will never be hired again. The LA Young Guns will never give us money. They can rot in hell. And we need to go back to the plan where you raise the money you promised."

He sat in silence as he tried to figure out how to convince me to hire Jack back on. After about two minutes of silence, I walked out. I called my lawyer, but we still didn't have anything to take legal action on. I spent the day trying to figure out what they were really up to. I suspected that the LA Young Guns were going to give Mickey the twenty million that they had allocated for us. That way, Mickey could save his failing meal kit delivery business (the idea he'd pinched from me), merge our brand with his, and then flip the entire entity for a profit. It was all just speculation, and everyone said I was insane. But it was the only thing that made sense in my head.

A couple of days went by and the stress of the situation was so thick in the air you could cut it with a knife. Everyone was speculating what was going to happen with the new investor group and how we were going to move forward with these people in our lives.

And then, a miracle.

One of the main investors of the 1.2 million Mickey had raised was the heir to a retail chain. He was a raging alcoholic and woke up every day like it was a brand-new world. I had been receiving emails all week from the investors asking about Jack and the health of the business, but then I received one that was just a forwarding of a chain. It was forwarded by the retail chain heir to about ten people, some I knew, and some I didn't. The email asked the group: "What are we going to do here about Jack? Are we still on track for Q1?"

I scrolled down the email chain to see what this email was referencing and quickly realized I was not supposed to be on this forward at all. The forward consisted of about forty emails between those who put money into the 1.2 million, plus Mickey and Jack. Mickey and Jack had been telling investors they had already taken over the Tessemae's board and were in complete control of Tessemae's, that the Vetters were no longer working there, and that the money they were raising was a bridge to the LA Young Guns. It was exactly what I had thought they were going to do—steal our company.

Everyone was copied, all the information was there, and the proof was in the pudding—or, in this case, the forward. And so, I also forwarded it . . . to my lawyer with the opener: "I fucking told you, motherfucker." My lawyer immediately called me in shock. "Greg, I mean . . . I can't believe what I am reading. This is the most insane thing I have ever read. Thank God you didn't sign anything."

Yes! I was right. But my satisfaction was short-lived because my lawyer had something else to say.

"But we need to do a rescission offer to the 1.2 million investors that they brought in, or you are in deep shit."

What's a rescission offer?

My nightmare continued.

## Field Guide: Lessons Learned

### What You Need to Know
Hope will kill you.

### How to Do It
Prepare for the worst, plan for reality, pray for the best . . . knowing the best is probably not coming. And if it does, chalk it up to a Christmas miracle. The minute I stopped thinking a miracle was going to come and save me was the minute my life changed for the better. Stop waiting and hoping. Start reframing your mind to battle for the long haul.

### What You Need to Know
Train like a warrior that runs through storms.

### How to Do It
Prepare every morning to battle. Map out what "winning the day" looks like and what it's going to take. Get visual with it. Prioritize the day in time slots and attack each task like you are a mercenary. The more efficient and methodical you become in this approach, the more productive you will be. The more you mentally prepare to run through the storm, the easier the run becomes. Don't plan for 72 degrees and sunny with a slight breeze. Plan for a hurricane.

### What You Need to Know
There is only trust.

### How to Do It
TRUST: It's everything. I should have never gone back on my universal law of "when someone breaks my trust, they are dead to me." How you do something is how you do everything. If someone can't be trusted, that carries through to everything

they do. Don't ever make excuses for their lack of character or trustworthiness.

Your gut knows all. Those feelings you are getting in your gut are real. They are trying to tell you something. Your brain will try to rationalize it away but don't do that. The gut knows when things are bad or something is up. It's probably one of our last animal instinctual traits we can still rely on. When the gut speaks . . . listen.

# ELEVEN

At some point in every young entrepreneur's journey, you stop doing the fun stuff.

The fun stuff, in my case, was making salad dressing, designing the brand, developing new products, and coming up with ways to scale the business.

When the fun stuff stops, you become the one thing you were trying to avoid all along: the "suit for hire."

I felt like the suit had caught up with me and swallowed me whole. I had not focused on anything fun in almost a year. Ever since we decided to raise money after the PMA Summit, I had been dealing with the bullshit of money raising, lawyers, and finance assholes. And now, I was dealing with new forms of bullshit that I didn't even know existed, like rescission offers.

## Unraveling the Lie

A rescission offer (I learned the hard way) is when you formally give the money back to investors in a legal process that voids their investment because they were sold a lie. Lawyers run point on the execution of the process so everyone is notified of their rights, the reasons for the rescission offer, and the different scenarios that are possible should investors stay or leave.

Tessemae's rescission was for 1.2 million—for the investors Mickey brought in to buy out the bank loan. And there wasn't much time to make it happen. If it was hard to find money for growth, (which it was) it was even harder to find money for a rescission offer. NO ONE wanted to be a part of that shit. We had to sweeten the deal to get people to participate. We made the note secured, gave the investors a four-times return on their money, and paid them interest until they were paid back. The only people to step up were our board members. There was Paul, a successful lawyer, Ivy league graduate, who got involved with us for the adventure of being part of a start-up. He was a partner at a major law firm and saw himself as a partner on our journey. And also stepping up was our other board member Brendan and an early investor who liked idea of protecting his equity investment with a secured note.

All the payments had to be made at the same time, all the documents had to be signed on the same day, and then it would be done. It was basically like a giant home closing with a title company, but way more complicated.

We set up a separate account to hold the cash, so we didn't fuck up the process. Just setting up the bank account with the proper lawyer access and visibility was a pain in the ass. This was a weird moment for me because all of our time and effort wasn't focused on growing the business or raising money for the business; it was focused on getting people out of the business that should have never been involved. Everyone was dragging their feet about raising money for the rescission offer because we still needed to grow the business. It was a bizarre distraction that could not be avoided. And even though it was painful and annoying, we knew that if we left Mickey's crew in our company as investors, they would eat us alive from the inside out.

The cash came in with a week to spare, and everything was on track to pay off Mickey's group. I spent that entire week on the phone with Mickey's investors explaining what had happened, and I waited patiently to see who would stay and who would leave. It turned out that the entire group that invested with Mickey did so with the plan to take us over and flip Tessemae's for a giant profit. No one wanted to stay. So, the entire 1.2 million would be deployed on Friday to pay them off.

Wednesday evening of the payoff week, my phone rang. It was our controller, Timothy. Timothy never called me, especially in the evening. This was a guy who had retired from a career as a corporate controller, and he was pretty sure he'd seen it all. He joined us because he thought it would be fun to be in an entrepreneurial environment. When he spoke, he took a very calm approach, with no sense of urgency because he didn't need one. And he didn't work a minute past business hours. So, when my phone rang in the evening, I had a bad feeling.

I picked up the phone, and the first words out of his mouth were: "Greg, I fucked up." Did he ever. He'd incorrectly planned the cash flow and spent $300,000 of the rescission money. "When will the $300,000 be back in?" I asked. He didn't know. Best guess: one to two weeks.

So much for hiring "experienced" executives. This one had royally fucked up at a critical moment. I hung up the phone and called our lawyer to get information from him, hopefully without setting off any alarms.

"Is there any way we can bump the payoff to next week?" "Absolutely not," he said. "If you don't pay them off Friday, the rescission offer will not happen. Why do you ask?" I made up some bullshit that I was cash planning to try to get more product out of the door and hung up.

Who in the fuck could give me $300,000 in twelve hours? It wasn't like our situation was awesome and we were giving someone a great deal. We were captured by pirates and about to walk the plank.

I called Brian to talk through who we could call, and the only person we could think of was Edward. Back in college, Brian went to Barcelona with Edward, a guy who turned out to be a billionaire. There was a movie made about his dad, and they now lived on 3,000 acres in Malibu. We both agreed he was the only guy in our elaborate and sketchy imaginations who would potentially loan it to us on such short notice. Brian called him, and twenty minutes later, we had a deal. Edward said, "Pay it back to me in two weeks, and I'll loan you the cash."

Edward for a win that cannot be described in words. All we had to do was get the cash in by the next day and pay off the rescission offer Friday morning.

I went to bed in a daze because every day was this way—dramatic, catastrophic, and mentally draining. It was like we had leveled up in the arcade game Galaga and no one told us how the game worked. You are just this lone ship that can only move left to right and shoot your weapons at the "problems." They start off slow and it seems that this game is easy and fun. But each problem you solve is followed by new problems that get a little faster and more aggressive. The next thing you know, you are feverishly pounding the shoot button while aggressively moving this tiny joystick back and forth as hard and as fast as you can. And then you eventually die—Game Over.

I didn't want to go out like that, but I couldn't help but think about the insane shit I had been going through on a daily basis and thinking about how much faster and bigger the problems were getting. I went to bed that night praying that the Edward money would come in and the rescission would be executed.

I woke up to an email from Brian saying Edward's wire would hit when the banks opened in California. I waited and checked my phone every minute until the wire hit, and it did. Thank the fucking lord! We could now properly execute the rescission on Friday and put this chapter of chaos behind us.

It was bittersweet to send out the money for the rescission notes. We should have never been in that position. Timothy should have not fucked up the cash. Edward should not have had to wire us $300,000 at the drop of a dime, but that was life for us at that time. We were living Joseph Campbell's "Hero's Journey," but I still didn't know what stage we were on.

The board and our lawyers were happy that it had all gone "smoothly," and we focused on the next obstacle in front of us, which was getting rid of the merchant cash advances. "Onward and Upward" was the note Partner Paul sent me that day. I never had the heart to tell him and the rest of the board about the $300,000 fuck up by Timothy. I honestly don't think their hearts could have taken any more chaos in that moment. None of them had signed up for this level of bullshit when I asked them to sit on the board. They were in it for the same reasons as Timothy; they thought it would be fun to be in on this entrepreneurial journey.

## Onward and Awkward

Since Timothy could no longer be trusted, I fired him that Monday. The bright side of all that rescission darkness was that it allowed us to set up a factoring arrangement with the sketchy Georgia bank. Because our first bank loan was paid off and the three investors that put up the 1.2 million were now our secured creditors, the Georgia bank could take the "first position on AR," which allowed us to factor our purchase orders. In Buddhism, they refer to this level of suffering with a positive ending as "the lotus in the mud." Sometimes the way to a solution is not how you thought it would be, but you still get there.

To think that the level of suffering was going to be my new normal made me rethink how I was approaching life in general. I needed to be able to endure unbelievable amounts of chaos and stress while remaining focused and clear. I read *Shoe Dog*, the memoir by Nike founder Phil Knight, three times that year, trying to learn little ways to make it through the chaos and prevail. Some lessons applied, some didn't, but engaging with his journey gave me hope that my story could have a happy ending as well. The one thing I knew I had to do was begin to only focus on what mattered. I literally didn't have the brain capacity to experience anything other than that. I wrote out what a "perfect day for me" was. *Wake up early, write, meditate, read something of substance, work out hard, see the sunrise, see my beautiful children and wife, laugh, cry from joy, work toward something of purpose, watch the sunset, eat dinner as a family, go to sleep knowing you did everything you could that day to be the best version of yourself.* And that is still what my perfect day looks like. Prioritizing those little but important things allowed me to maintain happiness, clarity, and focus.

Removing all the bullshit also allowed me to be more productive in a day, so I could try to solve my problems. The dressings and salads were doing very well, but the business was not profitable because of the infrastructure we built to support our growth, coupled with paying 35 percent interest on three million and 20 percent on a mountain of investor payments. We were paying about $300,000 a month in loan payments, which gave us no room to fuck up. We had to be perfect and focused, or the entire house of cards would crumble to the ground. The past year's efforts had only given us a life raft, but we were far from being rescued. We were still in the middle of the ocean with no food or water.

I sat down with Brendan to figure out how we were going to find three million during the holidays before the company stumbled again. Brendan is a very unique dude. Enlisted in the Navy straight out of high school, became a Navy SEAL, was asked to be on SEAL

Team Six for multiple years, and then he came home and worked with his brother as a personal trainer. In working with his brother, he started training Henry, the founder of a Fortune 500 business. Henry thought Brendan was smart and paid for Brendan to go to business school. Once Brendan the SEAL was done with business school, Henry, who was one of Tessemae's earliest financial backers and controller of one of Tessemae's board seats, asked him to run his home office. That's how Brendan and I met.

As we sat in the conference room mapping out how we were going to solve the problem of raising more money, he looked very stressed. To lighten up the mood, I said, "This may be bad, but at least we aren't dealing with what SEALs have to deal with, right?" He looked at me and, with a serious tone, said, "This is way worse, man. When you're a SEAL, you're trained to do a job and everyone is the best. If there's a problem, you solve it. This shit we're dealing with right now? Dealing with people's paychecks and livelihoods? This shit is stressful. And there's no way to solve these problems easily." I raised my eyebrows in surprise and then said, "OK, well, don't tell anyone that because I have been using that comparison a lot with people in the company, and everyone seems to calm down when they imagine being compared to a Navy SEAL." Brendan chuckled, and we went back to problem-solving.

By the end of the meeting, I had lightened Brendan's day, and we left the conference room with a "hit list" of people we were going to try to raise money from. The next morning, I ran into a guy at the gym who was a business acquaintance, and he asked how I was doing. I always answered those questions relatively honestly because you never know who can help, so I said, "Not great. I'm getting the fucking shit kicked out of me, and I need to find some debt to get rid of these merchant cash advances." He said he had a buddy who used to be a president of a bank and now ran a private lending platform for businesses, and he would introduce me.

We scheduled a meeting with the buddy—a guy named Ryan—and went to lunch. I explained the situation, and he was very receptive and said he could help. At first I thought he was going to just loan me the money, but it turned out he was going to set up meetings and then try to collect a finder's fee. The first meeting Ryan set up was with a guy who literally looked like Gollum from *Lord of the Rings*. I am not fucking kidding you. Same hair, same translucent wet skin, this dude looked like he was dying, but when you are in the depths of hell, you don't really get to pick and choose who will potentially give you a lifeline, so Gollum it was. Gollum came to the manufacturing plant for a meeting, tour, and to try the products. The meeting was going well, and as we went back to the conference room, he started asking us if our vendors were important to us. "Why?" I asked. "Because we are going to put you into a prepackaged bankruptcy and clean up this shit show."

Shock, confusion, silence, and then I managed a response. "Yeah, I'm not doing that at all, so if this is your plan, you can leave right now." He was stunned and tried to backpedal on the bankruptcy word by giving me additional options he could bring to the table to invest in the business. But it was no use, every solution dealt with bankruptcy. After flopping around for another twenty minutes, we said our goodbyes and parted ways.

## Hearing the 'B' Word

Everyone left the conference room, and I went back in to sit alone. Bankruptcy. That was the first time I had heard that word during my Tessemae's journey. Is that where we were? Were we bankrupt? Were we a shit show? I knew the past year was hard, but was it this bad? I drove home defeated and in silence. I tried to gather my energy so my kids wouldn't see me looking like a weakling, but Genevieve knew something was up. I told her what Gollum had suggested, and she had the same reaction I did. "No way, Greg. You can't give up like that." I agreed with her and told her I would fight to the end, but what else was there? I had been told "no" for seven months straight, lied to by an existing investor, slandered in the Baltimore business community, had to execute a rescission offer, which could potentially be the last dollars I raise, and all of that to meet Gollum from *Lord of the Rings* to declare bankruptcy. All that shit for fucking bankruptcy? Fuck that. But was bankruptcy the lotus? It didn't feel like it. I tried to stay focused on solving the problems of the day but needed to go to bed early. It was almost as if my body was shutting down to protect me from exerting any more energy so I would be prepared enough to attack the next day.

I woke up at four and sat at my desk, trying to write my morning pages to get my mind prepared for the day but couldn't write. I just sat there in the dark, stressed beyond imagination. Was this the end? Was my dad going to lose his house? Was I going to lose my house? Was this the dumbest venture any idiot had ever embarked on? It had been over a year since the PMA Summit, where we experienced the highest high I had ever felt in my life and now I was at my lowest low. Funny how time can change things. And as I sat there thinking about the day's monumental list of tasks and never-ending obstacles, I couldn't help but wonder if I was going to die from stress in that very minute. *"Can you die from stress?"* I thought. *"If you can, and it happens like a heart attack, this would be the moment."*

I wrote some thoughts down in my Moleskine, put my pen down, and waited to die.

As I sat there with my eyes closed listening to the silence, there was nothing. Just the ringing of silence in my ears and the slow and steady thumping of my heart. My mind was blank, and it felt like a complete void. After about five minutes of hearing my strong heart not giving in, I came to the realization that I wasn't going to die from stress on that day, and the only option I had was to solve my problems and put this chapter behind me. I finished my morning pages, meditated, and went to the gym.

I was a different man after that morning. And perhaps a part of me did die at that desk. I was slowly becoming hardened and losing patience with all the unnecessary bullshit I was dealing with. I also realized I was alone and that no one was going to help me solve my problems except myself. So, it was either win or lose. The old adage of "when it rains, it pours" looked more like waterboarding all over my soul. Shortly thereafter, Genevieve reminded me we didn't have money for Christmas that year. We piecemealed things together that gave the impression that things were OK but they were far from OK and getting worse by the minute. I tried my best to radiate joy and presence for the kids, but each day was a slog in the fucking muck.

## Working with the Worst

Ryan sent me three more groups to meet with to be potential lenders, but each group was worse than the last. Apparently, the easiest thing to do in complicated times is just fuck everyone over and take the entire thing for yourself. Well, I wasn't interested in doing that and voiced my concerns to Ryan regarding the groups he continued to send to me. Ryan was tall, with a gentle voice and a very loose handshake, and hung around the worst human beings in the world. I didn't like the people he was sending me but had no other alternatives. The only thing we could potentially do were more merchant cash advances, but that would have just made things worse. I was beginning to lose hope and then Ryan suggested that his own capital group loan us the money.

My first thought was: Why didn't you just do that in the beginning? But then I realized there must be a reason he is doing it now versus in the beginning—what was it? The initial reasoning was that he allowed four separate groups to do all of the diligence on the business, and they all came back with the same conclusion: The brand is awesome, the product is awesome, and when Tessemae's gets out of this shit show, they will be awesome. Ryan's capital group was the equivalent of a loan shark, and in true scumbag fashion allowed other people to do the work so he could make the money.

The only issue with Ryan the Shark's deal was they wanted equity for the loan, which required 100 percent of the investors to sign off on the deal. So, we started making calls to investors about Ryan the Shark's proposal. Last the investors had heard from us, we summarized the rescission and plans for growth. Their reactions to the rescission were not great, so I knew this new news was going to land like a cinder block. The calls were all the same for the most part. They were pissed: "How did we get here?!" But they all signed off on the deal. Except one, Jerry Blue Eyes, the Marine, who had been brought in by our seed investor, Tom. Jerry would not sign off on the deal because it changed the interest payments on his investment, and he wasn't going for it.

I tried to talk to him, but it didn't go well. We had Brendan try. Still no go. I was furious. Brendan agreed with me but reiterated the point that Jerry was a holdout. I called Ryan the Shark to see how much they cared and if there was a workaround.

"No. Jerry either signed, or the deal was dead," Ryan stated.

We tried to work Jerry Blue Eyes for a week with no movement. Closing was set for Friday, and Ryan said that if Jerry had not signed off by then, he was moving on. Thursday night, Brendan texted me that he was going to give it one last shot with Jerry. I didn't hear from him for over an hour and now it was 10:30 p.m. I texted Brendan to see if everything was OK and no response. I paced nervously around my house, staring at my phone, waiting for a call. At 11:30 p.m., Brendan called me and said, "We have Jerry's sign-off." I'm not sure if Brendan went over to his house "SEAL Team Six style" or what happened, but the signature was there.

I texted Ryan the Shark that everyone had signed off, and on April 20, 2018, I signed the very aggressive loan papers for three million to be repaid over a two-year period with 20 percent interest and 5 percent equity in the business. The interest would be split: 12 percent being paid monthly and 8 percent being "paid in kind," otherwise known as PIK. As I read over the papers, the only thing that kept popping into my head was: *Live to fight another day or die now.* I signed the papers in the test kitchen with everyone watching me. Whatever I was signing had temporarily saved our lives and allowed the Tessemae's journey to continue, which everyone was elated about. And as I signed the documents, I smiled and started swiveling my hips like when Forrest Gump met Elvis at his mom's bed-and-breakfast. Everyone laughed and celebrated. We scanned the documents and sent them over.

The money was wired shortly after and the merchant cash advances were paid off. I had bought myself two years until this level of stress would be present again in my life. But for this moment, and at least the next month, we had enough runway to take off again. It turns out that when you don't have throat-choking interest payments sweeping your account every day, a lot can get done. I got back to work on growing the company and stopped worrying about the lights getting shut off.

## Field Guide: Lessons Learned

### What You Need to Know
Trust your gut and follow your core life values.

### How to Do It
Write down your beliefs. What are your tried-and-true values that have never let you down? Make a mission statement for yourself and list out your core values. Then take all of that information and create a filter for making big decisions that incorporates your value system. In moments of inner conflict, when your gut and brain are at odds, ask yourself why. Then run the decision through your filter. And then if you are still having inner conflict, ask yourself what you are choosing to ignore about the situation. You will find clarity there.

### What You Need to Know
You must evolve faster than everyone else around you if you are to maintain the ability to lead by example.

### How to Do It
The easiest way to evolve faster than your peers is to find a mentor that has actually done big shit and is willing to give you ruthless unfiltered advice. If you can't find a mentor, create a reading list of great people who you respect and learn from their lives. Take notes on each book you read and write a book report. At the end of each book report, apply your favorite principles to your own life and make a "recommendations brief" to yourself. What areas of the leader's life did you like and why? What habits did they have that you don't currently have? What would be the easiest way to implement those habits into your life? That simple act will allow you to create a growth plan for yourself so you can become the leader you want to be.

### What You Need to Know
Prepare for all your biggest fears to be realized and put on display for the world to see.

### How to Do It
Joseph Campbell has a great quote "The cave you fear to enter holds the treasures you seek." Mine was bankruptcy. I did everything in my power to avoid it, and rightfully so. That decision should not be made without serious thought. But I put myself through massive suffering to avoid it at all costs, which made the situation worse. Surround yourself with people who are not emotionally connected to your business and are experts in the subject. They will give you insight that you don't want to hear, but it is most likely correct.

# TWELVE

With the restructuring of all the merchant cash advances and unsecured notes, we were saving over $300,000 a month. It was fucking awesome. There was this sense that we had been tested to the very edge of where a man could go and didn't quit. And because of that, we got to go back to our normal lives of growing the business again. We had been moonlighting as investment bankers, emotional support dogs, and tour guides in hell for a year-and-a-half and it was nice to get back to waking up without the alarm clock of panic.

We started growing all aspects of the business again. Everyone's mood was lighter. Everyone smiled more. Everyone was back in the mindset that we could actually build the next great American consumer packaged goods brand. But I knew I needed to get a jump start on raising money again if I was going to get a good deal and not be pressured into a shitty scenario like last time.

### Food for Football

That summer, a news program aired a story about an all-black Baltimore private high school that was so good at football that the rest of their private school conference in Baltimore wouldn't play them. Every team would forfeit their game against Holy Spirit for "safety" reasons. Safety reasons in football? This can't be real. But after watching it, the arrogance and delusion of the parents and teachers from the other schools clearly spelled out the insane lengths people will go not to be embarrassed. The interesting thing about Holy Spirit was that the school was located where a lot of our manufacturing workers were from, so we asked a couple of the guys in our warehouse about the Holy Spirit team. "Oh, yeah! They play their games on Friday nights. Shit is sold out, and there is basically no crime during the game cuz we're all at the game!"

That seemed like a group we wanted to meet. Genevieve tracked down the coaching staff (she should have been in the CIA) and then scheduled a meeting with my dad, who had been running our non-profit arm, to talk to the team about clean food. My dad decided to just drop in on one of their practices in the 'hood of Baltimore. He strolled on up. "Hey, Coach Fred! I'm Steve Vetter with the Tessemae's Foundation. Genevieve called you." Coach Fred and his staff looked at him in complete shock. "What are you doing here? I thought we would meet at the office or somewhere nicer." My dad chuckled. "Nah, this is fine. I've been all over the world, and these places aren't that bad once you get to know the people."

The area where Holy Spirit practiced was in one of the worst parts of Baltimore. The previous season there was a drive-by shooting when they were practicing, and everyone had to lie on the ground until the machine gun fire stopped. It's not a nice place by any stretch of the imagination, including my dad's. We call it the Zombie Apocalypse, and to see big Steve Vetter walking up there without a care in the world set the tone with the Holy Spirit coaching staff that we were not fucking around.

My dad explained to Coach Fred that we wanted to help their team from a food, nutrition, and performance perspective and were willing to donate either food, time, or both. Coach Fred explained what they currently had for tailgates and pre-game meals, which was basically nothing. The tailgate consisted of a piece of candy, a lunch box portion of Pringles, and a mini bottled water. And the pre-game meal did not exist.

My dad reported back, and we were in fucking shock. One of the top high school teams in the country and they have no food? How good could they become with good food? We wanted to find out how we could be the most impactful for the team, so we went to the first game of the season to catch a vibe. The stands were fucking packed. The team was unbelievably good. And at the end, the tailgate consisted of a couple of moms handing out plastic baggies with Pringles, a lollipop, and a mini water as they walked to their team vans. It was nothing. It was almost less than nothing. No celebration, no one hanging out and talking. I thought back to my own playing days, when my mom would bring her famous homemade salad dressing to the post-game potluck meals we had. The Holy Spirit team deserved better than some Pringles while walking to the parking lot.

We came back to Coach Fred and his staff and outlined how we wanted to help. The first piece was the tailgates. We would fully orchestrate and execute the tailgate for all the home games. The second part was general nutrition planning and education for the guys to understand how to build muscle and eat like an athlete. And the third piece was identifying and screening the guys for any preventative risk markers based on body composition. We brought in the strength coach, who had been training Team Vetter since the three of us were actual athletes, and had him look at the kid's foot structure, knees, body comp, and movement patterns. The Holy Spirit staff was shocked. "Why were we doing this?" I finally replied, "Because we can. I love nothing more than a David vs Goliath story, and I understand the journey of trying to turn nothing into something. I fucking love this shit."

Everyone was appreciative of our effort. For the first tailgate, we brought enough food to feed a small town. The team went from a piece of candy and four Pringles to salad, bread, pasta, meatballs, and dessert with four coolers of drinks. Not only did the kids eat, but all the coaches, parents, and random fans that stayed around got in line as well. We set up a giant assembly line and served everyone, explaining what that night's menu was and how proud we were of the team's victory. They all smiled ear-to-ear and were very grateful. The guys got to experience what a post-victory tailgate was: hanging out with family and friends and celebrating your victory. That's what many high school and college kids do after games. And now they got that as well, and they loved it. Each week was a slightly different menu, but centered around refueling a bunch of growing future D1 animals.

## Money Quest, Take Five

Around November of 2018, I wanted to get the ball rolling with the money raising. The deal with Ryan the Shark's capital group had been done for about six months and the business had regrouped and was thriving. The numbers were strong and growing, and it felt like it was time to get an early jump start on "the bullshit," aka money raising. I called Coach Fred to see if he knew of a good investment banker to use since he had an investment fund of his own. "Why do you need an investment banker?" Coach Fred asked. I explained our past financial follies. He asked a couple more questions and then said, "I'll send my guy down there Thursday to walk through what you need. He's the best." Well, that was easy. We already had a lead on an investment banker to get the ball rolling. This was good. We set up the facility and conference room for our normal tour process, which included a tasting of all our dressings, a menu centered around the dressings so everyone wasn't just sitting there drinking salad dressing out of a paper shot glass, and a tour of a very clean building. We would bump up the music, so when people entered the building, they immediately knew they weren't in Kansas anymore.

But as a car pulled up, it wasn't just Coach Fred's guy, Barney, that got out. It was also Coach Fred, his son, and one of his investment partners. Interesting, I thought.

Bald Barney was my age but looked thirty years older. He had lost all his hair from stress, his skin hadn't seen the sunlight since he was 16, and he was always glistening from a constant panic sweat that consumed his life. He was the perfect minion for Coach Fred.

We took them on the tour of the facility and showed them how the dressings were made. They met all the people in the building, tried all the food, and as we were walking back to the conference room, in almost the same exact spot where Gollum asked me the question about bankruptcy, Coach Fred said, "What if I just give you the twenty million?" I looked at him like he had spit on my mother. "What?" Coach Fred continued, "This is what I do. Why don't I just give you the twenty?"

I processed what he had said and looked at him to see if he had said what I thought he said and replied, "Let's go talk it out." We walked back to the conference room and went over what the future looked like. At the end of the presentation, Coach Fred asked everyone to leave so we could sit together and talk through what a deal could look like. It was a very honest and informative conversation, and we both parted ways with some homework to do to see if we wanted to do a deal together. I was still very gun-shy from the number of broken promises and backstabbings I was healing from and knew we needed more than one horse in the race. But, regardless of the past pain, I was excited to have someone interested in the money raising that we could potentially trust.

After the meeting, I synced with my brothers, Genevieve, and the rest of the team and explained Coach Fred's interest. Everyone was excited to almost be out of hell, but I explained that we needed other options to make sure we were actually going to get out for good. Brian called his college roommate, who was high up at a New York investment bank, and asked him about potential avenues for the twenty million. The roommate connected us with the Growth Debt Fund of the company. We set up a call and walked them through where we were, why we needed the money, and where we were going. They said they loved the opportunity and wanted to be in the race.

Now, one of the ongoing problems that finance people always had with Tessemae's was that we were always growing. Things were always happening, and it was hard to take a snapshot in time and then build a financial analysis process around that moment. We were a "bowl of spaghetti" for these finance nerds to sort through which they did not like. And this time was no different. The Big Box Retailer salad business was getting bigger, and the entire "fresh" side of the business was growing with opportunities by the day. We had convenience stores requesting "fresh grab 'n go" options for their stores, the branded dressing packets in the Big Box Retailer salads had grown a once-stagnant category by 34 percent, and colleges and universities were talking about bringing in the grab 'n go options for their athletes. All pistons were firing, and the energy of the business had shifted to "white flame" hot.

But all that growth in dressing and produce didn't change the other problem that finance nerds had with Tessemae's: salad dressing isn't sexy. The interesting thing about the *fuh-NANCE* space is that they are all mini-clones of one other. Same colleges, same grad schools, same internships, same four banks, and then they split off from there. For all intents and purposes, they are the same. They are basically the Minions to Grube. That's why they all get wrapped up in the same dumb trends. They think the same. They are risk averse. They are nerds, and they have FOMO. So, if one of the risk-adverse analysts says something is "hot" or the space is "sexy," they all jump in. Salad dressing has never had that moment and never will.

Regardless, the business was growing, and people were interested in us. As the football season continued, and we continued to support the Holy Spirit football team's nutrition needs, I got a front-row seat into what I thought was an inside look into Coach Fred's character and his team. I didn't want to have another LA Young Guns or a Mickey's Marauders on my hands. So, I was not rushing to get married. But I only saw the good side of Coach Fred because of all the winning. The football season ended up being magnificent. They beat their biggest rival. They were ranked #2 in the country and went down to a bowl game in Georgia and destroyed the #3 team in the country at their home stadium by forty points. Winning has a funny way of bringing out the happiest in people.

But I continued to try to get a deeper understanding of Coach Fred as well as the New York investment bank guys. The New York guys were very straightforward. They were the most risk-averse, slow-moving *fuh-NANCE* nerds you have ever met. I started to think the only reason they were entertaining this deal was because they loved talking to me and my brothers. We were like a sitcom to these dudes. I am sure you have figured out by now—we don't have a filter. They loved talking to us, and after a while, it felt like a complete waste of time. We were their break in the middle of a boring day, where they could hear us sling cuss words and see people laugh.

As the new year was upon us, the business was in its busiest season, and I wanted to get term sheets in the door and make decisions. The New York group was hesitant to send one over, and so was Coach Fred's crew. Everybody wants a great deal except the person giving it and this was where the rubber met the road. Coach Fred gave us an overarching structure, but we needed something more formal, and the New York guys kept kicking the can down the road. This went on for a couple of months, and then we had a board meeting at the end of April. That was the deadline for when everyone needed to make their decisions.

The Growth Debt Fund deal was no equity, just expensive debt, and the Coach Fred's deal was all equity with a board seat. The business was growing aggressively, and in that moment, the equity value was increasing by the day. Our board wanted to do the debt deal, so I called Coach Fred and let him know. "Really? Alright, bye," he said. I've had longer calls with a bill collector. I knew he was pissed that he didn't get the deal, but the board valued the equity more than the cash to service the debt. Then, I called the Growth Debt Fund and started pressuring them to make some moves. *What else did they need? When was this going to close? If we are going to do this, then let's do it!*

## The Blame Game

While all of this was going on, there was an internal power struggle involving Tessemae's VP of Finance, our CFO, and our Head of Sales. They were all jockeying for the title of Head Finger-Pointer in The Blame Game. I've said it before, and I'll say it again: Big corporate types can't grow small companies. There is too much responsibility, accountability, and visible consequences to your actions. No one from a corporate background wants that shit. They want the glory from the win with a deal day tee shirt and a pat on the back.

We had a metrics meeting every Thursday where we went over the entire business based on the department head's key metrics. And at this stage, each meeting was turning into: *"It's not my fault. If (insert other department here) would deliver what they said they were, then we could properly (do our jobs) (Insert additional excuses and recriminations here.)"*

I don't do well with finger-pointing. One of our core values is literally: No excuses: Before you point the finger, point the thumb. And this behavior was reaching a boiling point. Unlike Victor Frankl and his teachings from *Man's Search for Meaning* in which you have perspective and awareness from your struggles so you can find peace in the *now*, this crew had taken an amnesia pill and forgot what we had just overcome. And my tolerance for bullshit was at a zero. The summer was cranking, and we were launching a bunch of new products for Back to School in 10-oz dressing bottles, as well as two new salads at the Big Box Retailer. There was a lot of innovation happening, and all the while, the rest of the business was still growing. The need to be dialed in on your shit was at an all-time high. The Growth Debt Fund was continuing to kick the can down the road and asking for the same shit over and over again. And every time something new would happen, like a new salad at our Big Box Retailer, they would need updated forecasts, and the process would start all over again.

We set a deadline for the Growth Debt Fund's final proposal for July 3rd, and we were all marching toward that deadline. Then we received a call from one of the Growth Debt Fund clones. "A buddy of mine who used to work for this fund has a private equity fund in Texas, and we want him in on the deal. He is flying in Wednesday to take you all out to dinner, is that cool?"

Hmmm, but this was a debt deal, not a private equity deal. If I wanted a private equity deal, I would have gone with Coach Fred. But I was willing to sniff them out. "Sure, let's meet at this restaurant in Baltimore, where my friend is the chef, and it will be great." But I was not sure this was great at all. My "time kills deals" detector was rising fast, and it felt like this was the Growth Debt Fund's way to get out of our deal without having to say no.

The Texas crew came in, and they were all nice. We had lots to talk about, and they said they would send over a proposal on what the equity structure would look like if they were to participate. Sounded good enough. At a minimum, we could have an additional baseline value for the business and use it to our advantage. A week later, the proposal came over, and it was fucking shit. Just total shit. They valued us like a pawnshop would value a fake Rolex. I was pissed. I called the Growth Debt Fund and said we weren't doing that deal but we're willing to do that structure if they had someone that was willing to see the value in the brand.

They sent over a couple more "home offices," but those guys moved too slowly. They had no reason to move quickly because the decision-makers were working with money that was just sitting in the bank. Home offices were not a fund. They were investors of cash they'd already made. So, their goal was simply not to fuck it up. By about the third call with home offices, I was getting pissed. This was supposed to be a debt deal, not a complex debt and private equity deal with multiple partners. If they didn't want to do the debt deal, I wanted them to just tell us, and we would move on.

## Coach Fred Is Back

We were still marching toward the July 3rd deadline, and the Growth Debt Fund said they still wanted to do the deal, so our finance team kept making them forecasts that took into account every possible variation of circumstance including a slight breeze coming up from the southeast.

I hadn't heard from Coach Fred in a while and then he popped up in the news because Holy Spirit's schedule was released for the upcoming year. I sent him a note wishing him well because we were still going to help with the football team's food needs. The bridge wasn't burned with him or his team; it was just under construction. He replied back asking how I was doing, and we chatted a bit over text, and then he called me. "What's up, stud?" I answered, "Just dying in a desert from thirst while the Growth Debt Fund sits next to me with a water bottle, analyzing the correct angle to pour it into my mouth." He laughed, and we went on to chat. He asked if he could stop by the manufacturing plant to say hello that week, which I agreed to.

A couple of days later, we were sitting in the conference room together shooting the shit, and at the end of the conversation, he asked if there was anything he could do to help. I jokingly said, "Become the Growth Debt Fund and give me the debt deal my board approved." He looked at me and said, "Are you serious?" I replied back, "If you are. The debt deal was approved by my board because there was no equity. Why don't you take that deal, get paid interest, and then have it convert in the future at a predetermined amount? That's the best of both worlds. I get what I want, even though it's more expensive, and you get what you want."

He gave me a side-eye and shook his head like he was in. The next week he called me and asked for an updated forecast, which I had in every variation one could imagine. I was the fucking Baskin Robbins 31 flavors of forecasts. I sent them over, and he called me back quickly. "Call the board and see if this is cool before I start rallying up my troops again." I called the board and let them know the fish I had on the line, and they wanted to be assured the Growth Debt Fund was, in fact, not going to do the deal like it was previously pitched to us, meaning only debt. I called the Growth Debt Fund guys and told them about the situation with Coach Fred and how we needed to get a very clear understanding of how this deal was going to go down and by when.

On July 3rd, the Growth Debt Fund sent their "final final" term sheet. It was a mix of debt and equity. The debt amount was way lower than previously discussed and was sliced into three segments. The equity component required a lot of operations oversight and board representation. It was almost a deal so bad you couldn't find a way to do it. I initially didn't say no. I took it to the board, and we discussed all the changes the Growth Debt Fund had made and then discussed what we would accept from Coach Fred's team. We all agreed we needed to find out what the Coach Fred deal looked like with all the new "wins" under our belt, so I called Coach Fred and told him the board was getting frustrated with the Growth Debt Fund, and if he acted quickly, it was his deal to lose. He said he needed to get with his team and get back to me. But all things were pointing in the right direction.

As Coach Fred's team began to dig into our models, I was scheduled to take a vacation to Rehoboth Beach with my entire family—my brothers, all the kids, my parents, and random friends who were going to be there. But I knew I was going to be distracted. I told Coach Fred & Crew that I was available if he needed to chat, but there would probably be kids screaming in the background when he called.

## I Left Them Alone for Five Minutes . . .

About a week into the vacation, I received a call during the regularly scheduled metrics meeting. "Hey, Greg, you have the entire team on the call," said my CFO. "The forecast is off this month, which means the cash is off, and now that we have a better handle on the forecast, we aren't going to have any money to launch the innovation for back to school."

Furious but silent, I let everyone speak. And the finger-pointing began. The finance team was taking the position that it was all sales' fault. The sales team was taking the position that the forecast is hard to predict and it is what it is. The ops team was siding with the finance team and everyone started blaming the sales guys for their lack of ability to predict the future. After about five minutes of back and forth, I lost my shit. "How fucking dare you. Blaming someone else without taking any responsibility at all. Suddenly, it's your team vs the world? Just give me the fucking facts of what we need and cut out all the bullshit!" There was a long pause, then one of the finance team members spoke. "We need a million dollars by Monday if we want to launch the salads on time."

I hung up the phone. What in the actual fuck. A million dollars by Monday? Are you fucking kidding me? Everyone was inside our vacation house, looking through the window at me screaming in the middle of the street, and knowing something bad was happening. I went on a walk to try to come up with a way to find one million dollars at a moment's notice. After about three blocks, there were only two names: our board member Partner Paul and Coach Fred. I didn't want to call Coach Fred because that could fuck up the larger deal, so I called Partner Paul first to get his thoughts and hope for a miracle. He listened and then said, "Well, you are going to have to figure that out, Greg." I knew that was going to be his response, and honestly, it was the right response for his position. He had just saved Tessemae's by stepping up during the rescission offer, and he didn't need to do it again. A man can only save another man so many times. And so, I was left with one option—Coach Fred.

The risk-reward promise of this avenue was not great. But I had no other options. I sent Coach Fred a text to call me when he was free and then went to the liquor store to buy enough alcohol to kill a fraternity. As I was loading everything into my car, Coach Fred called. "What's up, stud?!"

I dove right in. "Hey, my man, I just got a call that the two additional Big Box Retailer salads are at risk if we don't buy raw materials on Monday. If we don't make some serious moves here, these salads aren't going to launch."

"How much do you need?" he asked.

"A million bucks by Monday."

"OK, let me see what I can do. I can't promise anything, but I will let you know either way by tomorrow."

The call went better than I'd expected, so instead of drinking away my sorrows, I drank to celebrate a small victory.

The next morning came around, and no word. I didn't want to harass Coach Fred because I knew it was a long shot, so I just waited. I did my normal post-drinking routine, which was twice the level of workout, to squeeze the organs clean of the poison, and then distracted myself with beach time with the kids.

By three o'clock, still nothing. Fuck man, this isn't going to happen. And then at four-thirty, a text: *call me*.

Fuckkkkk. This doesn't sound good. I got Coach Fred on the phone. "We will do this million dollars, but we aren't committing to the larger raise yet. This is a one-off deal, and the terms are going to be shitty. But if you accept the terms, the money will be there Monday."

I thanked him for his quick turnaround and told him I'd look at the offer right away and get back to him. The terms were shit, but fuck it, more salads in the Big Box Retailer and strengthening that relationship vs quibbling over nickels. I accepted the terms of the deal, and the money came in on Monday. I was still pissed about how dysfunctional everyone had been while I was gone for five days. On my return, I called an all-hands-on-deck meeting to let people know there would be no more tolerance for mental weakness or "culture cancers." We had been through hell and were supposed to be battle-tested. "I didn't forget how much we have overcome, and I certainly don't take it lightly that you are still here fighting the good fight, but if you think making it to this point gives you some sort of free pass to be an angry piece of shit, you are fucking dead wrong."

The message was well received for the most part, and we got back to growing the business with a more "aware" outlook. But there was still the Coach Fred big deal to be closed. The money from Ryan the Shark's capital group was due in April of the following year, and it was August. Based on how long it took to get to this point, I was starting to pick up my pace and sense of urgency, so I wasn't backed into a corner again. I needed to get this shit closed before Thanksgiving, or odds were it would never be done.

## Field Guide: Lessons Learned

### What You Need to Know
True character is everything.

### How to Do It
Get deeper than someone's surface-level character. You need to figure out who they actually are. A great way to get a glimpse is to go out to dinner with the person and their spouse. How do they treat the waitstaff? How do they treat their spouse? See them in an uncomfortable situation. How do they react? What additional signs are there that you are ignoring? Are they put together? Are they fit? Are they a slob? These are all signs that will help paint a picture of who this person actually is. Take those moments of "real" character and compare them with the surface-level character they try to portray.

### What You Need to Know
Understand when people are broken and need to be relieved of their duty. The person will not tell you since they will most likely not know.

### How to Do It
There will be signs of behavioral change. A once positive and upbeat person will now have a shorter fuse. A generally optimistic person will now see the glass half empty in every scenario. A once unstoppable salesperson will be tired and hesitate. Address the situation with the person head on and then observe. They will initially "shape up" but the test will be their behavior two or three weeks later. What do they fall back into? Do they fall back into their old selves or their new broken identity?

# THIRTEEN

Coach Fred & Crew were now our partners for at least one million dollars. I was grateful that he acted on such short notice, but I also understood there was a cost to that action. The cost was most likely his doubt in me, and the viability of the team set in place.

But it was a risk that had to be taken. September was upon us, and there was a lot going on. New products were launching in the Big Box Retailer. Condiments were launching in retailers. I was still working on raising money with Coach Fred, and the timeline to get the raise done was getting shorter by the day. I needed to get a better understanding of how long it was going to take to close the more expansive Coach Fred deal. But it was easier said than done. Fred would give me one answer, and then his minion, Barney, would give me another one. The information was vague and contradictory, and I felt like I was trying to herd cats.

On top of all this, our national grocery chain called and asked us to present all our innovations at their annual innovation summit at their headquarters. For years we had been showing them bits and pieces of our innovation pipeline, and now they wanted to see it all. At the time, we had some cool collaborations going on with Jerry Garcia and Laird Hamilton, so we decided to pull out all the stops and bring everything we had.

OK, I know what you are thinking: Why would we present MORE innovation when we could barely manage what we already had in production? The answer is easy. We did it because we never wanted to be the guys who were satisfied. We were always reaching for the stars. I was always in search of the Nike Air Jordan—the product that could change our stars and truly put us on the map. And I always felt like we were *right there* on the cusp of that happening. Maybe it was going to be Laird's Superfood line of dressings? Maybe it was going to be Jerry Garcia's Cosmic Jerry Sauce? We were a good company, but I wanted to be great. In business, you are either growing or you're dying, and I always choose growth. This event would be no exception.

The R&D and Sales teams got together and started mapping out what we would present, and I got back to the never-ending Coach Fred deal. It was now at a standstill without a revised term sheet from him. We were talking multiple times by phone a day, but it felt like a Growth Debt Fund situation all over again, where he just wanted a break in his day so I could make him laugh. I was starting to get somewhat concerned as we entered the end of September but invented reasons in my head as to why the deal had not been closed.

*It's football season. Coach Fred is distracted. He will get around to it. I just spoke to him yesterday. This will all work out.*

But I knew that time killed deals, so I shifted my urgency to the sales team as a strategy to grow our way into investors' hearts. Everyone loves a winner, and if we could get a couple of big wins under our belt, investment from the outside would be easy.

I kept Coach Fred's team up to speed via email on all the innovations we were presenting to the grocery chain and how our bid for additional Big Box Retailer business was going. I couldn't be distracted by any more calls that ate up my time and never seemed to get the right information conveyed to his other partners. This "lost in translation" loop was getting old. Email and text were good enough tools, and besides, we had some big opportunities that needed our focus. I could not afford to continue as Coach Fred's lunch-hour entertainment. I needed to give him more to love than my natural comedic genius.

## Money Quest, Take Six

Brian and I flew out for the innovation summit with everything we could think of. We had Laird's superfood dressings, Jerry Garcia sauces (with or without CBD), multiple BBQ sauces named after Vetter family members, new wild dressing flavors like Sweet Chipotle Ranch, and marketing materials for all the buyers. As we were pulling up to the building, Coach Fred called. I almost didn't pick up the phone because I was in Game Time mode. But I did anyway. I listened for a while and then said, "Deal."

Brian asked what happened. "Coach Fred just gave us the terms of the twenty million equity deal: Forty million pre-money valuation, 15 percent paid interest on the cash until it converts, and one board seat. I told him: Deal."

We both smiled and gave each other a big, complicated handshake that you see athletes throw on ESPN. Brian was pumped. "Fuck yes! This is fucking sick! Best news ever before we go dominate this meeting! Let's fucking go!"

I called our board members Partner Paul and Brendan the SEAL and quickly told them the news as we entered the building and walked toward our meeting. Then, Brian and I proceeded to dominate the meeting and secured some more shelf space in our existing set. It was a good use of our time, but now we needed to execute on multiple fronts: The Coach Fred deal and growing the business.

Coach Fred's team sent over a structure when I got back, and we began negotiating the terms. Once the details were ironed out, Bald Barney sent the final term sheet over—with one major red flag. It was for seven million, not the twenty million I'd said "deal" to. I called

Bald Barney to see if it was a clerical error, and he informed me that was all they were doing. I was pissed. All the negotiations on board seats and controls were based on twenty million, not seven million. I called Coach Fred for clarity, and he punted the responsibility to Bald Barney and said it was his call to make. "But it's your money! And what happened to all that your word was your bond and the deal was done. And when I say a deal is done, it's done. Remember?!"

He told me I could come up to Holy Spirit and talk to him face-to-face, which I did immediately. I fucking U-turned into oncoming traffic and got up to Holy Spirit in thirty minutes—a drive that would normally take forty-five. We met in a classroom in the basement, and he sat in one of the desks like a little kid about to get scolded, even though I was the one about to get bad news. I stood the entire time, pacing, and he looked down the entire time, jumbling his words, trying to explain why they didn't live up to our original deal. But the long and the short was they were only in for seven million dollars, and that was that.

This was not good news. I called the board, and they were fucking pissed. Partner Paul wanted to walk away from the deal because of "this man's lack of honor." But we decided to at least get the seven million in to buy ourselves time while we began the search for another partner. So, I got out my tin cup, put on some Chapstick, and went back out into the money-raising world for the remaining thirteen million.

As I was interviewing investment bankers, all communications from Coach Fred's team stopped. It started to feel like the seven million wasn't going to come in either. There are multiple immortal truths in this world, but the two that were ringing in my head were: Time Kills Deals and Behavior Is Consistent. This deal was taking too long and Coach Fred's excitement and behavior had changed. It was now the beginning of November, and I knew we were entering the last possible moments to get anything done. Nobody does anything during the holidays in *fuh-NANCE,* and Thanksgiving was a couple of weeks away.

One of the traits that has kept our business alive all these years is our forward progression. We never stopped moving forward, no matter how bad it got. Maybe we only moved an inch one day, but it was an inch forward, and then we would hold the line with everything we had. *Fortitudine Vincimus—Through endurance, we conquer.* So, we kept grinding to hit our goals no matter the circumstances. Now we didn't really have the money to accomplish our big goals for the next year without investment, but I would cross that bridge when we came to it.

Partner Paul was now furious at the Coach Fred & Crew. "How in the hell could a grown man say something, shake someone's hand, and not live into his word?!" It blew his mind, and his stance remained firm: abandon Coach Fred & Crew and find the money somewhere else. But I kept hounding Bald Barney for the seven million. In my mind, thirteen million was easier to raise than twenty million. And if we already had a partner in hand for the seven million, that should make it easier to get additional partners.

I sent Bald Barney an email asking about the seven million and the timeline. His response was: "You should move forward with a formal raise."

What the fuck did that mean? Was the seven million coming in or not? Was all of that time wasted? Was I going to be put into a corner again and forced into some horrible deal? One year wasted. All that time and work, for that guy to say no. It's not even his fucking money. But that's how it goes in the money-raising world.

This was bad news. It was November. The holidays were coming, the loan from Ryan the Shark's group was due at the beginning of April, and I had nothing to show for my effort as we headed into the new year.

And if there wasn't enough chaotic shit going on, Brian sent me a text that said he is moving to California. California? For what? "I like the vibe out there, and I can be closer to the produce business," he said.

So, to recap: Coach Fred is a flake. The money we shook on may or may not come in. It's November. I am hiring an investment banker—again. Brian is moving to California for . . . I still don't know why, and Ryan the Shark's money is still due in April. Great. I thought again about my favorite twist on an old saying: *When it rains, it waterboards you.*

## Holiday Doldrums

It was now mid-November, and the holidays were basically upon us. You always know when a holiday is coming because everyone stops promptly answering emails or picking up the phone. But I kept grinding for some sort of win. We were still waiting on an answer from the Big Box Retailer on the Master Kit business we'd bid on. Each salad contract was worth about nine million, not to mention the salads would have Tessemae's 1.5-oz packets for the dressing so it was free advertising. We were supposed to get the answer on who won the contracts at the beginning of November, so as the dates zoomed by this wasn't looking promising. No news was bad news. I started to rationalize not getting the Big Box Retailer business. *I mean, it's almost better that we didn't win the contracts because we needed Coach Fred's cash to buy the raw materials, and that cash was nowhere to be seen. And so now we can focus on dressing.*

But I knew that wasn't true.

I was starting to get as stressed as I had in 2017. I needed to control what I could control and stop worrying about areas I had no control. But I couldn't stop asking myself: *What is Coach Fred going to do? When will Brian move? Who will be our new investment banker?*

*Would we raise the money in time? What will happen if we can't pay Ryan's group back by April?*

I needed clarity so I could problem-solve, but all I was doing was worrying. And worrying was doing nothing except making me stressed. I sat up one night writing about the journey with the hope of finding answers in my cobwebbed brain. I started with all my problems, but then I found myself writing about all my blessings. My life was amazing, and I was allowing outside factors to negatively affect my mind. I pulled out the quote in my wallet again: "The ultimate measure of a man is not where he stands in moments of comfort or convenience but where he stands in moments of challenge and controversy."

I was doing a little better than 2017, so there was some growth, but I needed to take control and be the man I knew I could become. I wrote out a promise to myself and signed it:

"It seems like everything has reached its breaking point. It feels like every decision we make is going to be something big . . . and then it never is. And each failure leaves you feeling like you are moving backward instead of growing from the pain. I need to give the company an update on where we are going and how things are progressing tomorrow. Do I still know? What if there is only right this second, this moment? What if all I am is resolve, resilience, perseverance, grit, endurance—The true test of a man's character is not where he stands in moments of comfort and convenience but where he stands at times of challenge and controversy. How am I handling that test? Where are things going to go from here? I don't know, but all I have is right now. All I have is this moment. What do I need to do right this second to pass the test? You get what you deserve. You are where you are meant to be. I will stand strong and press on. I will do what needs to be done. I will be the living embodiment of that quote and pass the test. I will lead by example. I will put faith into the journey. I will not waiver. I will be the husband Genevieve needs me to be. The father my children deserve. The brother I know that I can be. The son my parents knew I would be. The leader I set out to be so long ago. God, Give me the tools and the capacity for greatness. Give me the ability to be the man I set out to be as a young boy and the man we've all been waiting for. Allow me to accomplish my dreams and live up to my promises. Protect my family, our health, love, happiness, and this journey. Give me strength."

The next morning, I woke up in peace. I don't know why, or how. Nothing with work had changed. Things were actually in more flux than they were the previous day, but I had come to the realization that this journey was happening FOR me, not TO me. Whatever was happening, no matter how bad, was going to happen as a part of the natural life cycle of this business. And I accepted it as a personal challenge.

I met with some investment banking firms, and they all said the same thing everyone says: What a wonderful story. Amazing how you did that. You guys are going to raise money no problem. But from us, it's a no.

To say I didn't have much faith in investment bankers was an understatement. But I decided I didn't feel like dealing with their bullshit until the new year. No need for unnecessary distractions during the holidays. On Friday, November 22nd, we had a board meeting. It was also my mom's birthday. I wrote in my journal all the things I was grateful for and then prayed for a miracle. The board meeting agenda was not looking good. We didn't make payroll that week, no word on Big Box Retailer contracts, no word on Coach Fred's cash, no decision on an investment banker, and the only news we had was bad news. I was prepared to fight my way out of this meeting.

As I walked in, you could tell everyone was annoyed and frustrated about the situation. How much more bad shit could one salad dressing company take? We walked through all the issues and all the upside but people were emotionally burnt out. Partner Paul and

Brendan the SEAL were hanging on by a thread, and it felt like this journey was coming to an end. I walked out with a laundry list of action items that the board wanted to address: We needed a hard "yes" or "no" on all our pending bullshit, so we could start focusing on where the business actually was and stop talking about all the "what ifs."

I walked to my car, a little defeated, and began driving home. I called Genevieve and gave her an update on the board meeting. She always worried about me in those things, so "proof of life" was always my first order of business. As I was ending the call, Brian called. I expected this. He'd want to get his usual update on how the board meeting went and to see if we still had jobs. I picked up to give him a rundown of the meeting, but instead he shouted, "Five Master Kits, motherfucker!"

"What? What are you saying?" I asked.

"We got the Master Kits with the Big Box Retailer! It's worth thirty-six million dollars! We ship in January! LET'S FUCKING GO!"

Brian was screaming. I was in shock. We just locked in a thirty-six million contract with the Big Box Retailer?!

I called Genevieve back and told her the good news. She started crying and was screaming, "Yesssssssssssss! We did it!"

I sent a text to the board with the good news, and they were fucking shocked. They actually didn't believe it and just kept saying: "Well, we will see." Yeah, we will see. Accept the win!

As I was driving to pick up my kids, I was in a daze. It was a miracle. An actual miracle. All the kids piled in the car, and we headed home. As we were driving home, Coach Fred called. "I'm wiring three million right now, and my associate will wire the other two million Monday." Confused, I asked, "What do you mean you are wiring three million right now? Why?" "Because I said I would. You still want it right?" Coach Fred asked.

Laughing, I said, "Yes, please."

I called Brendan the SEAL to tell him the news, and he said Bald Barney had just called him. "So, you are telling me we get five Master Kit contracts and five million in cash on the same day? Within two hours of each other? Holy fucking shit." We both laughed and celebrated the moment. I couldn't believe it. I drove home and hugged Genevieve. We all celebrated that night because it was my mom's birthday but also because we had just experienced a real miracle. I woke up the next morning and prayed: I gave thanks and gave gratitude. I couldn't believe it.

## Prepping for the Big Box Launch

As the next few weeks rolled by, I still had trouble believing what had happened. We won the Big Box Retailer contracts for the family-size salads. It was such a far-fetched win that I needed proof, so I would read the award letters on a daily basis to make sure I wasn't making it up in my head. After reading the award letters, I would call Brian as a joke to double-check. "We still have those Big Box contracts, correct?" Brian would laugh and reply, "Yeah, dumbass, stop calling me about this." But it was just too outrageous to think about how far we had come. Who in the fuck were we to win something this big? We were making salad dressing in a fucking "meth tent" the last time I checked. Now we are a produce company with one of the largest retailers in the world?

The board didn't believe the win was real. All they kept saying was, "Well . . . we will see it when it happens." And I would remind them, "It's happening. Stop bringing negative energy into my fucking miracle." But I never let them put any doubt in my physical actions. I was running forward like Indiana Jones with the boulder on his heels. I was convinced that taking action and bringing the salads to life with perfect execution would be a sign to the universe we meant business.

Now, winning the contract was one thing; actually delivering on orders of that scale was something totally different. The board and our California produce partners were full of doubt. The Tessemae's crew and Coach Fred were the miracle believers. Just the simple act of winning the contracts had officially solidified our "X factor" to Coach Fred's team that we were different—that we were special. We were the combination of *The Bad News Bears* and *The Mighty Ducks* leaving sports and going into business. We may look like public school pieces of shit, but we win when it counts, no matter how big the miracle needs to be.

As the Big Box Retailer salad plan was being implemented, I wanted everyone completely locked in on our priorities. Each day, I would send out an email with a quote, our main priority for the day, and the time until Master Kit blast off. And just like a rocket launch, we checked and double-checked every detail we could control on a daily basis prior to blast off. As the moment approached, we decided we needed to send out our "execution team" to California for two weeks leading up to launch. The last thing we were going to do was fuck up the biggest opportunity of our lives.

Brian ran point on the operations execution team in California. The team was a mix of Tessemae's operations people and some new hires we took from the produce partner. Brian was not really an operations guy, but he was fucking ruthless, and that is what that moment required. We had no time for minced words or office politics: it was ship or don't come home.

As the team left for California, the magnitude of the opportunity began to sink in. We were going to be a legit produce company now, not just some salad dressing startup. And it wasn't just the produce contracts that were creating the magnitude of the moment; it was the fact that we had branded Tessemae's salad dressing packets in every salad. Millions of new consumers were going to experience Tessemae's dressings for the first time.

Oh, and did I mention that Chef Kristen had invented shelf-stable ranch dressing? So, when all those new consumers from the Big Box Retailer decide to go to their local grocery store and peruse the salad dressing aisle, Tessemae's would be there for the very first time. Now, we didn't invent shelf-stable ranch dressing, that has always existed. But no one had ever figured out shelf-stable, clean ingredient, no thickening agent, delicious, organic dressing. And we were happy to be in that aisle. It addressed one of the most common questions we were asked: "I went into the salad dressing aisle and couldn't find your stuff. Where is it?" And we would reply: "That's because it's in the refrigerated section of salad dressings . . . with the lettuce."

It usually fell on deaf ears, but we continued to battle it out in lettuce land. Until we received a call from the global buyer.

"I was just in our annual buyers meeting. The main topic was disruptors, and you were the case study on salad dressing. They ended the meeting and said: GO FIND YOURSELF A TESSEMAE, and I thought, why don't I just call Tessemae's and have them make shelf-stable salad dressing . . . duh."

And that is how our shelf-stable dressing was born. Sometimes, you need a sign, or in our case, an uppercut.

Everything was finally coming together in a way that felt like it was meant to be. We didn't want to waste our "moment" so we started brainstorming on how we could capitalize on the good fortune. The Big Box Retailer contracts were amazing, and the shelf-stable dressing was a game changer, but we still needed people to know who Tessemae's was. We were very popular in niche markets and "food tribes," but we needed the average American mom to know we existed. We decided it was time to explore an advertising campaign.

## Tessemae's Meets *Mad Men*

Coach Fred's friend owned a big marketing agency that specializes in large-scale, comprehensive TV ad campaigns. The founder's son, now a professional actor, launched his TV acting career by appearing (for free) in all of his dad's commercials. We met with the marketing agency and told them our rollercoaster of a story. Their jaws were on the floor. By the time I told them of all our adventures, they wanted to work with us. No surprise on my end. This outfit spent most of its time doing commercials for hospital systems and hotel chains. We were giving them the opportunity to take a break from the ordinary and date a "rock star." We asked them for a comprehensive plan and estimate of what it would cost to make Tessemae's better known in the wider consumer community.

They decided on a comprehensive plan of national targeted digital ads, commercials on Pandora and radio, with a three-region test of TV in markets that had the following criteria: major grocery chains that carried all our flavors—refrigerated and shelf-stable dressings. That narrowed the options down quite a bit because we had just launched the shelf-stable line. Yet, there were enough regions that had everything we needed, and we settled on the Pacific Northwest, the Southwest, and the Midwest.

We wanted it to be fun, different, and impactful. Every food commercial at the time was a family or friends sitting at an outdoor table having a big happy meal laughing in slow motion with a narrator talking about clean ingredients for the people you care about. We needed to cut through the noise and make people listen. The initial idea we settled on was: "Flavor you can't ignore." The campaign was pretty funny, very bold, and could work. It was giving every flavor a hilarious personality that would talk to the person eating the food. Think Balsamic sounding like Wanda Sykes and Cilantro Lime Ranch in the style of Spicoli from Fast Times at Ridgemont High.

We went through the initial build-out of how all the campaigns would cohesively work together while they got TV advertising rates for our selected regions. It came back to be three million for a little under three months of airtime. My eyes bugged out. "Three million! HOLY SHIT, America better think these dressings are funny as fuck." The marketing agency promised the campaign would be executed well, and I told them I would follow up with my answer. Coach Fred had asked to come to the final meeting with the marketing agency to see if the campaign was going to work. After the meeting ended, he called me and said he would put in the three million to make that ad campaign happen. "Greg, this is going to work. This is genius. Call them right now and say it's a done deal."

I was pumped—our first national ad campaign! I called the marketing agency and gave them the green light. Coach Fred was now in for eight million when we thought he was going to be in for ZERO. Not bad for persistence.

Genevieve and her team ran point with the marketing agency, and the next thing we knew, she was sitting in auditions for voice actors. The shoot took place in Atlanta, Georgia, over the course of a week, and we flew the marketing team down there for the full experience. Genevieve, Moe, and their marketing squad absolutely loved it. They were sending pictures back to us left and right, sitting in the director's chair and taking pictures with the actors. And when they arrived home, they felt like they had a winning product. But was it three million good? Was it good enough to give us a return on our investment? It was a lot of money, and we weren't in a place where we could just blow three million and get nothing for it.

But that was my bullshit to worry about, not theirs. They needed to continue to focus on launching the ad campaign in unison with the Big Box Retailer Master Kits and the shelf-stable dressings we were calling the Pantry Line. The plan was to bombard consumers in the three regions with Tessemae's. The Big Box Retailer, grocery stores, radio, TV, digital—everywhere they looked they would see Tessemae's and imagine each flavor's hilarious character. But the strategy only worked if we shipped the Big Box salad kits.

Spending three million on media is always a risk, but this was especially risky because the money was from a new investment partner and the kits had not yet shipped. All bets were on numbers that had not come to fruition yet. We knew the ad campaign was going to help the brand regardless, we just didn't know how much. And the one factor that was still beyond our control was the Big Box Retailer situation. Were we going to be able to make this thing happen? Were we really going to flip a switch and have an extra three million a month in sales? The award letters said: yes. My heart prayed: yes. But our journey had taught us to be skeptical. And the board was firmly in the skeptical camp. It was just too good to be true, and they couldn't wrap their heads around it.

I didn't hold their negativity against them. We had been at the "first and goal" mark for years but kept getting stopped. It felt like we were in some form of hell or purgatory. And heaven was right behind the gate. It was so close we could touch it.

C.S. Lewis wrote an amazing book titled *The Great Divorce* about this concept. We could see it, we could go there, but we had to do something that we hadn't figured out yet to move on. Our arms stretched out, yearning to cross over, but moving in slow motion. Would we ever get there? That was us in the two weeks leading up to the launch. Everyone was waiting for the other shoe to drop and to find out that this thing we had all been banking on wasn't actually real. I kept waiting for the call from the Big Box Retailer. "There was a mix-up. We sent you the wrong contract. Yours is worth nothing." But I kept that doubt to myself and tried to keep everyone focused on executing the plan.

Brian had his work cut out for him in California. We would talk daily about the issues he was having, but he was taking no prisoners.

I guess one of the keys to our success is the fact we are willing to make anything happen no matter the obstacle. The folks out in California were not like that. An issue would come up, and they would say: "Welp, that's it, guys, guess this isn't going to work." Brian would tell them: "Shut the fuck up and solve the problem." We would chat daily and go over all the scenarios where people were "stuck" and the best ways to get them "unstuck." And inch by inch, day by day, we were getting closer to blast off.

## 5-4-3-2-1 . . .

On February 26, 2020, the Big Box salad kits shipped.

We all looked around and didn't know what to do. We called all the distribution centers to make sure the product had been delivered. We double-checked with the Big Box Retailer to make sure everything was to spec. We promised each other we wouldn't celebrate until the money arrived, but we were now "first and inches."

And then the first Big Box check hit. We had done it. A thirty-six-million-dollar contract with the Big Box Retailer was officially underway, and no one could believe it. I jokingly walked around the manufacturing plant congratulating everyone for doubling our business that day: "Thank you for doubling our business, and thank *you* for doubling our business. Congratulations on doubling our business . . ." Everyone laughed and enjoyed the moment. It was fucking surreal.

We all had some celebratory drinks at the manufacturing plant and tried to soak it all in. It was one of those moments you read about and imagine: *What would it feel like if that happened to me?* I can tell you from experience it doesn't feel the way you think it will. It's more relief than joy. The equivalent in exercise is doing a front plank for as long as you can, and when you feel like you can't do it for another second, when you actually feel like you might give yourself a sports-induced hernia, the timer goes off, and you get to relax. You are still in pain. You are still covered in sweat. You are still lying on the dirty ground. But the sharp, intestinal-wrenching pain of the plank is over. That's what it felt like to get a win of that magnitude. Relief of the pain of everyone saying we couldn't do it. Relief of the shackles from 2017 when we almost lost everything. Relief from the haters that said we would never make any of this work; and then the unbelievable gratitude of the present moment. A weight lifted off our shoulders. But once that relief fades away, it's not joy that replaces the relief in your mind—it's the realization that wins don't make up for the pain of losses. But you don't tell anyone that, you pretend that wins do have the magic to give you a clean slate, and you take that win, thank god, and try to get another one.

The board couldn't believe it and remained in shock for weeks. They would send me random notes: "Is the Big Box Retailer still doing well?" I would simply reply: "Yup," and that was it. As the Master Kits were shipping, the TV campaign was well underway, and the initial data we were receiving back was very good. It appeared that we had taken a wise gamble, and it was going to potentially pay off. For a split second, it felt like we were on the brink of "making it." We had the Big Box retailer contracts, shelf-stable dressing, refrigerated dressing, and TV commercials that were producing results. Stores showed an increase in our shelf sales of about 40 percent. No one could believe the results, including the marketing firm. They had never seen an impact like that so quickly, but we didn't want to get too excited. We needed more time to see what the actual impact was going to be over a three-month period. But the initial data got everyone hyped as fuck.

Coach Fred and his crew saw the numbers and put more money in. This time they committed to another eight million. They couldn't believe the advertising impact on the new Pantry Line and how strong the Tessemae's brand could be with the right support. A 40 percent increase in shelf sales of the refrigerated bottled dressing combined with endless opportunity on the Pantry Line, topped off with thirty-six million of the Big Box contracted money, made their opportunist boners get hard. Every aspect of our business was firing on all cylinders, and everything was going our way for the first time in a long time. We were having a moment.

## Field Guide: Lessons Learned

### What You Need to Know
All you need is one inch.

### How to Do It
This goes back to proper goal setting. What is your most important goal, "MIG," for the year? What are all the goals that roll up to that MIG being accomplished broken down to the day? When you know that your goals are correct and roll up to something of actual substance, you can accomplish something every day. You can take action on one goal at a minimum. You don't even have to accomplish it, but you do need to put your attention and action toward it. You can get an inch out of that simple task. And that simple action is forward progression.

### What You Need to Know
Go in the middle of the dance floor and set the tone.

### How to Do It
Take a deep breath, think through what the people want, and go give it to them. Don't worry or make eye contact with others. That will only make you hesitate. Create the energy that you want to receive back and people will come to you. We focus too heavily on waiting for the approval and opinions of others.

That's wasted energy. Take that energy and create so much value that you become the only thing people can see. In our case, it was locking in a deal of a lifetime with Big Box retailer that no one could deny.

### What You Need to Know
Fear is a liar.

### How to Do It
Write out your stressors. Write out your fears. Write our anxieties. And then look up the definition of anxiety . . . "fear of the unknown." Look up the definition of fear . . . "an unpleasant emotion caused by the belief that something is dangerous or a threat." And then realize that the stress caused by the fear and anxiety is all intertwined and all made up. When I went through that exercise and then looked at my life in the actual moment I was living, I realized all my stress was about future events that had not happened and probably wouldn't. Your job as a leader is to have clarity so you can make good decisions and lead by example. You can't do that in a state of panic. Put a quote on your desk or as your background on your phone and remind yourself who the fuck you are.

# FOURTEEN

I received a text from Ryan, our borderline-loan-shark lender, that he wanted to get breakfast at a nearby diner. Sounded fine and nothing out of the ordinary. We were on good terms, and we had the money to pay him off on time. And for the first time in a long time, I had plenty of good news to share in case he wanted a business update. We ate an oversized breakfast and shot the shit, but at the end of the meal, the other shoe dropped: Ryan the Shark said his partner was moving to Florida and wanted two million cash for the warrants instead of stock in the company. They were going to wind down the investment group, and the cash would let them go their separate ways.

I was a little taken back by the request but told him I would talk it over with the board and let him know.

But before I could respond to Ryan with the board's answer, we received a default notice in the mail from Ryan's group. I called our attorney. "Default? I just met with Ryan last week for breakfast and he asked for two million in cash instead of the warrants in the business. This can't be right."

Our attorney looked over the letter and said it smelled fishy. If we defaulted on the loan Ryan's group received an exit fee of 7.5 million instead of stock in the company. That's why the Shark was sending it.

Ryan knew we were about to pay off the loan and give him stock, but he wanted cash instead.

There was a thirty-day cure period to fix any issue that Ryan's group identified, so we decided we would pay off the loan two months early and incur the prepayment fee of $90,000. But when we went to wire the money, the group's bank account was closed. We called their office number. It was no longer in service. I texted Ryan multiple times asking what was going on, with no response. I called our attorney: "Is this a fucking joke?" Our lawyer laughed. "This is some crazy shit," he said. "We need to hire a courier to hand deliver them a paper check and take a picture of the exchange so when this goes to court, we can show the judge what was going on."

It took the courier about four days to deliver the check and send us the picture, but by then, the greed wheels were already in motion. Ryan's group smelled blood and wanted the exit fee. They made over one million in profit over two years from the interest on our loan, but it wasn't enough. They wanted instant gratification instead of stock.

The next letter we received from Ryan's group was a litigation notice. They were suing us for the 7.5 million because we defaulted on the loan. How? No one knew. We had to guess, speculate, and prepare for battle in court for a reason that was yet to be known.

## Meanwhile, in the Rest of the Company . . .

Outside of the litigation notice, everything was moving at warp speed. We had paid off Ryan's group on time and I made a mental note to put them behind us. From my perspective, it seemed we might just be over our money problems for the first time ever. The Big Box business was cranking. Tessemae's bottled dressings were cranking. The ad campaign was cranking. Our innovation pipeline was the length of a CVS receipt. We just needed to stay focused and not fuck up.

Brian was our Chief Growth Officer, and we would sync multiple times a week about the business. Most meetings were short and sweet but one week in early spring of 2020, he said this: "Everyone on the West Coast keeps rescheduling our meetings because of this flu."

## It Wasn't the Flu

Flu? Brian said he thought he'd gotten the bug months ago after a meeting with our produce suppliers in California. "I felt like shit, but it was over in a couple days. Clean eating, man, helps, I am sure." He promised to push the West Coast guys to stay on track.

Weird, I thought. The flu? I had gotten the swine flu two years prior, and that thing was no joke. But for *entire* businesses to be rescheduling for the flu seemed odd.

We focused our efforts on non-West Coast customers and kept grinding. The marketing agency compiled our results from the campaign and it was better than we had expected. In every region we tested, TV, mixed with radio and digital, our shelf sales increased steadily by 30 to 40 percent. The marketing team couldn't believe it. They recommended we take the same platform and do a national test over three months. To increase from three regions to the entire nation was only an additional one million dollars. We started to do the math on what a 30 to 40 percent increase in shelf sales would be across all our retailers and how we could use that advertising report as a sales tool to increase the number of products that retailers carried of Tessemae's. Could we get the entire innovation pipeline in all our stores? If we could do that, then the expense of the ad campaign would be irrelevant because we would have made it back tenfold.

We were ready to take the data back to the Big Box Retailer, show them how successful it was, and have them increase the number of Tessemae's products they carried. We had the script mapped out: "You carry six dressings and four salads. They increased by X amount with our ad campaign and generated X amount of money for you. If you increase the number of Tessemae's products you carry AND we continue with the ad campaign, Tessemae's will generate X amount for your company."

The sales team was pumped and started mapping out the sales strategy for all fifty-five retailers we were in. We were sitting on the winning numbers to an endless number of lottery tickets. We just needed to drive the winning tickets to the lottery building and cash in. Simple enough.

Then on March 5th, the country locked down.

Every retailer sent out notifications that they would no longer be taking meetings in person until further notice. To add insult to injury, our order cadence stopped as well. We received a note from a national retailer that said, "We need to focus on what really matters right now, and unless you sell eggs, milk, bread, or toilet paper, I don't care about you."

Was this for real? Were we really being locked in our homes for the flu? Every major news outlet was reporting on this thing like it was an alien invasion: "Stay in your homes. Don't go outside. You are all going to die." *Was I taking crazy pills?*

But I wasn't. People started flooding the grocery stores for hand sanitizer, eggs, milk, toilet paper, and water like it was the fucking end of the world. Grocery stores made those "critical products" their top priority regardless of what else was sold out in the stores. We would call and email the buyers to let them know we were sold out, but they didn't care. They were redirecting trucks to pick up eggs and milk. Trucks that pulled up to the distribution centers with anything else other than those critical items were kicked to the back of the line and told to wait. The stories we were hearing of truck drivers sitting outside of their drop-off points for days were starting to worry us. Unlike most brands, we had a manufacturing plant we needed to keep running. Orders weren't made at the drop of a dime, and the need to be nimble was more apparent than ever.

But the one area of business that never wavered was the Big Box Retailer orders. Every day, every week, the Big Box Retailer orders came in. For some reason, people were still eating family-size Caesar salads. That consistent ordering allowed us to stay alive. The 1.5-oz packets of dressing sitting in salads for a family of four kept the lights on. If we would have had to rely solely on the bottled salad dressing business, we would be dead.

The rhythm of our business was upended. There would be weeks with no response from our dressing buyer, and then they would order two-months-worth of dressing that needed to be delivered the next day. We would try to guess the cadence of the orders and then build around that guess, but that created an unbelievable amount of inventory. Sitting on that much inventory without any visibility into the future was also a death warrant. I never really understood what the saying, "stuck between a rock and a hard place" meant until I had to make these types of manufacturing decisions. We needed to protect cash so that we could protect our people and we had no idea when this "flu" would end. We had to control what we could control, which was basically Caesar salads, and only focus on finding wins. People were looking to blame someone for their problems, but there was no one to blame. We couldn't blame the buyers because they were getting destroyed. The buyers were basically living at their desks, trying to keep product on the shelves. You couldn't blame the raw materials suppliers, they were essentially in the same exact situation we were in.

And honestly, we were feeling blessed compared to our competitors. Most businesses that didn't own their own manufacturing were forced to shut down. Many brands who had gone with co-packers were regretting their decision as many of the partners stopped their production. Co-packing as a manufacturing solution quickly became the bonehead move of the moment. For the first time ever, private equity types were talking about how intelligent it was to own your supply chain. For years we were called idiots for not being "asset light," but for one year, we were geniuses. And not only was owning your supply chain important, but WHERE you owned your supply chain became more important. If you manufactured in California, you were fucked. But Baltimore—the beautiful 'hood of Baltimore—there it was all good. Why? Because our guys didn't give a fuck about this flu.

We bought two fifteen-seater transit vans and hired drivers to pick our employees up from their homes and drop them off every day. They loved it. We tested them every day for COVID-19, and no one got it. One guy had a "scare," but it turned out he went on vacation with his girlfriend for two weeks and wanted to see how long he could milk it. By week two, he forgot he was "sick" and started posting pictures on social media. We called him: "Buddyyyyyy, I thought you had Covid and were very sick?"

Silence . . . then: "Well, um, my girlfriend had it and then . . . nah, man, we went on vacation in Florida . . . I'll be back in two days, my bad."

The craziest part of COVID-19 was the massive divide between our HR people and the guys they were hired to protect. HR was freaking out: "How can we make these people come to work? It's barbaric!" But the vibe we were getting from our manufacturing team was the complete opposite. They had cars picking them up, meals provided, so they didn't have to leave the plant, flexible hours with pay, and they couldn't get fired for not showing up. We asked them if they wanted to shut the plant down so they could be "home and safe," like the TV news said. They all said nothing and started looking at each other. Two of them took us aside after the meeting: "Bros, this is some white people shit. We don't believe in it. We leave here and go to block parties until it's time to come back to work. You motherfuckers are trippin'. We have never been so happy."

We all started laughing hysterically and told them anytime they needed us to sponsor a block party, we were in! The plant never closed because of COVID-19 once. But those block parties led to some bad stuff for our guys. Our head of production, Jonathan, was quite the Ladies' Man. He was the type of guy that if a new woman came to work on the production floor—he was banging her on the side by the end of the week. Sometimes the women would find out about each other, and there would be full-tilt UFC fights to see who got him. We would always tell him: "Please, Jonathan, this is not going to end well for you if you keep banging other people's girlfriends." But he would just laugh and do his thing.

During COVID-19, one of his girls called him to help her move. He drove over on a Wednesday evening after work, but it was a setup. Her boyfriend was waiting for him and gunned him down in the street as soon as he got out of his car. The couple sped away and left him there to die. It shook our company to the core. He had been with us for five years, was about the same age as me, played football for a little while at University of Maryland, and now he was gone. As we got more details about the incident, it got worse. It turned out that an ambulance showed up, and he wasn't dead yet in the street. He made it all the way to the hospital before he died.

To think about this wonderful young man bleeding to death in the middle of the street alone emotionally broke our production team. About ten of our key production people couldn't come back to work for two weeks and then they just quit. They tried to come back a couple of times, but everything reminded them of Jonathan, and they needed to leave.

It was a bizarre tragedy to live through because the government wouldn't let you grieve properly. His funeral was live streamed because we couldn't congregate together in a church for a funeral due to COVID-19 restrictions. The plant navigated COVID-19, but we couldn't navigate Baltimore's hood.

## Money Quest, Take Seven

When COVID-19 began to become less dramatic, our business began to get more consistent. Many things began to feel like we were heading back to regular life, but we were far away from normalcy. All we could do was wake up and tackle the chaos of the day. Thank God we had the Big Box Retailer contracts to float the ups and downs of retail ordering. But even that couldn't last forever. We needed to protect cash, and we decided that one way to grab some easy money would be to jettison our sketch Georgia lender. The Georgia lender made money off every purchase order we received and would front us 60 percent of the cash that day. That system was important when we were only selling bottled dressing and not getting paid for up to sixty days, but now that the Big Box Master kits were cranking, we were getting cash in fourteen days or less. The produce business essentially replaced our need for the Georgia lender. We began the discussions to end the contract by giving them their required sixty-day notice.

As we were walking through a transition plan to leave them, they sold to a larger, even sketchier entity. The new company assumed all Georgia lender contracts and then superimposed their policies onto us and all of the Georgia lender's clients.

What that meant to us was this transition plan was now a hostage negotiation. They didn't want us to leave, and post-acquisition, they had a ninety-day notification period instead of a sixty-day. Not to mention a much more complicated pricing structure that was so vague, it was 150 pages long. It was the equivalent of being in a foreign country and someone handing you an encyclopedia in a language you didn't understand and telling you to give your family a tour of the book's listed historical sights. They tried everything to prevent us from leaving the relationship, but it was just too expensive to stay. We finally figured out how we could transition the relationship away and set up the date to pay them off. This was unnecessarily complicated because we had to notify all fifty-five retailers of the change, change our banking information with all fifty-five retailers, set aside the cash in a lump sum because they wouldn't allow us to slowly wean out of the relationship, and then pull the trigger on everything on the same day.

It should have been simple: New retailers start using the new bank, we pay off our sketch lenders, and move on with our lives. We orchestrated this hostage negotiation exchange on a Monday in the hope that when we were paid (usually on Wednesday and Friday), we would be able to seamlessly move to our new bank.

Monday, we wired them the 1.5 million to pay off the AR line of credit and said our goodbyes. But by Friday of that week not one retailer had paid the new account. We checked with the retailers to see if they had paid us, and it turned out everyone paid the sketchy bank again. MOTHERFUCKER. This was the opposite of Murdoch's quote from *The A-Team*: "I love it when a plan comes together." All that fucking effort, and it didn't work. But we didn't panic. Hey, it's only one week, and the sketchy bank will just send us the cash.

Not so fast.

We called the Georgia lender, and they said their policy in these situations states: "When a customer is no longer a customer, and they receive cash from a retailer, there could be a lag in the transition of cash back to a former customer of up to sixty days."

Excuse me? Sixty days! Sixty days of cash! Impossible. "We will be dead by then," I said.

Our finance and legal team went fucking berserk. But the new contract that we "assumed" when the Georgia lender sold to its new owner said exactly that. The Georgia lender's response was: "Well, you can come back, and everything will be fine again."

"Fuck that!" I said.

Maybe it was just one week of cash. We can survive one week. But the next week came and went, and still no cash in our bank account, only to the bank we were trying to fire. We went into DEFCON 1 and looped in the sales team. When you loop the sales team in, you are possibly negatively affecting the relationship with the buyer, which you never want to do. We were essentially "burning the ships." Our sales team called every buyer and had them walk into the finance office and read us what bank account they were paying into. Most retailers seemed to have the correct bank in their records. There had just been a delay in the physical accounting system switching over to the correct bank, but our sketchy bank was no longer on file. I allowed myself to think: "OK, this is going pretty well, we may just get through this."

But then Brian called. "I have bad news, dude. Big Box HQ never changed the bank account information, and they said it's going to take another two weeks to take effect."

My stomach dropped. I paused and then replied, "I don't care if you have to fucking walk to their headquarters and sit in the accounting team's cubicle yourself to solve this problem, but this needs to be done immediately! Or we are fucked." I asked Brian every question under the sun about how this happened and all that came back was the buyer just kept saying she hadn't gotten around to it.

Every dollar we had was now in limbo. It had been four weeks of producing product with zero cash to show for it. The sketchy bank not only had the 1.5 million we had paid to leave them, but they had two weeks of our cash and counting. All we could do was make a phone call, one I DIDN'T want to make. I had to call Coach Fred.

I told him our options: We could go back to the sketchy Georgia lender, and they will release the funds. Or we can wait it out. The only way we can wait it out is if Coach Fred & Crew gives us another three to four million.

He paused and then started peppering me with a million questions. After about an hour of interrogation, he said he would call me the next day. Defeated, I went to bed, hoping sleep would revive my soul. Coach Fred called the next morning around ten a.m. and always did a good job of sounding like he was on your side. "We can't go back to the Georgia lender. They are expensive and not good people. If I am going to keep putting money into this business on a moment's notice we are going to need more of a role in this business."

I listened, and we agreed that his team deserved a second board seat, which would increase the board to five. They get two, one independent, I get two. Once that was agreed upon, Coach Fred said he would send us the cash. "I'll wire you one million of it now and the rest by the end of the week."

Initially, I thought this was an amazing deal, and a crisis averted, but then Coach Fred's little minion Bald Barney called me right after saying he would send me a draft for the new money to review and then we would work through it. "Why would it be anything different than the previous agreement?" I asked. And he said it would just include the new board structure.

The draft arrived in my email, and it was insane. He was proposing that the three million buys him a board seat and an additional 30 percent of the business. I immediately called Bald Barney back and asked if it was an error before I decided to unleash hell. He explained it was not an error, and that was what he was proposing. "Is this a fucking joke? What kind of partner does this type of shit?" I yelled. He tried to go on offense and came at me saying, "This is market for this type of last-minute request."

I asked him, "Do you still live in Connecticut?"

He replied, "Yeah, why?"

"Because I'm getting a baseball bat. I'm getting in my car right now, and I'm coming to beat you within an inch of your fucking life in front of your family. I hope you're prepared."

He squealed back, "THIS ISN'T PRODUCTIVE," and hung up.

Coach Fred called me shortly after Barney hung up. "Did you say you were going to drive to Connecticut and kill Barney?"

"Yes," I replied.

"Can you call him and apologize and tell him you didn't mean it," Coach Fred asked.

"But I did mean it, and I will do it," I said.

Coach Fred chuckled. "OK, then just apologize so we can get this deal done."

"We can't get the deal done if what he proposed to me is true. That deal is fucking insane. I'll just go back to the sketchy Georgia lender and be done with this shit. You were the one that said you wanted to help me."

Coach Fred said he would call Bald Barney and circle back with me. Shortly after our call, Coach Fred texted me that they were heading down to see me at the manufacturing plant.

## Cue the Theme from *Jaws*

We met outside in the parking lot to keep social distancing and used the hood of a truck as our desk.

"Can you boys play nice?" Coach Fred asked.

"Depends what's on the paper," I said.

Brendan the SEAL, whom I'd invited to the meeting, interjected, "Of course, we can. Greg was just a little offended."

Bald Barney went on to explain that what he sent was a "template and a working document" that we would edit together, but the other members of Coach Fred & Crew just needed a signature on a working document to show that we were on the same page. I looked at Brendan with my eyebrows raised, and a face of "this sounds like a bunch of fucking bullshit." But Brendan said to do it. There were witnesses present, nodding that they understood that this was not the final contract. Maryland contractual law is grounded in "good faith business dealings." Both parties have to knowingly agree to what they are signing, or it's a "bad faith" contract that can be nullified in the courts, Brendan said.

I signed the document on the car's hood, and the other cash was wired over. My gut knew this was not good, and I knew this was going to open a can of worms, but it was that or die. Our bank account was now at zero, and we had no word from our sketchy bank.

But guess what: Bald Barney was lying. His fucked-up deal was NOT a template. It was exactly what he was proposing. When we began negotiating the contract with our lawyer the next day, he took the position that our mutually agreed-upon starting point was "the template."

All hell broke loose.

## Field Guide: Lessons Learned

### What You Need to Know
Go to the source for your information.

### How to Do It
Just ask the people directly. Get out of the boardroom. Stop watching the news. Stop asking experts. Go to the warehouse or your version of the warehouse and ask the people yourself. Getting real-time information from real people will always provide you with the clarity you need.

### What You Need to Know
No one is your friend.

### How to Do It
The people you think are your friends are acquaintances who are using you until you are no longer worth their time. I know this is a tough pill to swallow, but it's true. Never let a business

"associate" all the way in. Constantly revisit their character and loyalty to you and the cause. Once a year approach them like you are evaluating your partnership for the first time and try to look at your relationship with clear eyes.

**What You Need to Know**

Figure it out yourself.

**How to Do It**

Join the Young Presidents' Organization or a version of that. Discuss strategies with your peers who don't have a financial incentive to fuck you. Leverage every resource you can before tapping into people who are financially tied to you. Loose lips sink ships. The more information you give, the more vulnerable you become. The more problems you solve, the more valuable you become.

**What You Need to Know**

People are surprisingly worse than you can imagine.

**How to Do It**

I still keep a little faith that someone will pleasantly surprise me with their character. I do that by staying in the game and evaluating potential business partners by imagining a worst-case scenario. And then playing it out until the end. Then I make it 50 percent worse. What does that look like? Can you survive that type of onslaught? Can you withstand that type of attack? Every person who you let in your business increases your risk. The old saying of raising kids, "it takes a village," does not apply when you cross a certain threshold of business.

# FIFTEEN

The Bald Barney Template landed like a Scud missile.

Almost immediately, lawyers went to war, and they were all working off of this insane document instead of the discussions we had surrounding the document.

Even after all I'd seen, I was shocked. It's one thing to be greedy. It's a whole other animal to be greedy and a liar. Not only was Bald Barney holding firm that the parking lot document was our official agreement, but the only evidence we had against him were conversations we had in person, in the parking lot, over the phone, and in meetings. Everything we had in our defense was verbal. And we were fighting an enemy who had a piece of paper with signatures.

We circled our wagons by looping in our board, and that was a series of tough conversations. We had to go back to one of our earliest backers, Henry, Brendan the SEAL's mentor, who had made his fortune as an entrepreneur and invested in us early on. When Henry saw the Bald Barney Template, he was livid. "You motherfuckers are trying to fuck me out of my equity stake in this business? And you want my fucking help? I read the fucking document."

The battle, which was shaping up to be a faceoff: Coach Fred vs Home Office Henry.

The crazy part about their battle is that it was all ego. Neither one needed the money. But they were both Baltimore business elite, and Baltimore, no matter what the census may say, is a small town. Reputations were on the line. Each one was determined to outmaneuver the other. And the battleground was Tessemae's.

WHAT IS HAPPENING? To recap:

- Coach Fred was trying to steal the business for three million.
- Henry now wanted to fuck over Coach Fred for trying to steal the business for three million, which would fuck over the equity investors like Henry.
- Henry and Coach Fred now hated Tessemae's for involving them in the mess of the Bald Barney Template.
- Everyone now hated the Tessemae's management team for getting us all into this precarious financial situation.
- Our not-quite-a-loan-shark lender Ryan (remember him?) was still in the process of suing us for defaulting on a loan we repaid in full (and early.)
- COVID and lockdowns were still going on.
- The war between Russia and Ukraine had worsened a global supply chain crisis.

OK, moving on.

## Hunting for Solutions

As each party tried to maneuver to some position of strength, the other parties would find a new way to muck it up. The only thing that everyone could kind of agree on was that raising money to clean up the financial situation was paramount. I say "kind of agree" because Henry wanted to sell the company outright; Coach Fred didn't want to raise money or sell it but said he would go along with raising money if

Henry was not involved. I just wanted these assholes to stop distracting me and the management team from running our business.

As the parties began negotiating around which investment bankers to use and how much we were going to raise, our California produce partners (the lettuce guys and the onion guy) invited us to go hunting on Onion Guy's 25,000-acre private hunting ranch. It seemed like a good combination of business development and distraction from the never-ending bullshit of lawyers, so Brendan the SEAL and the Vetter Brothers headed out to go hunting.

Onion Guy is one of the country's biggest growers. Anytime we can get time with him is a good thing because he sits on most of the big produce boards in the country and when a commodity is needed for a Big Box Retailer salad, you want him on your side. Now his hunting ranch was in the middle of nowhere. No cell phone service, no Wi-Fi, no nothing. Just beautiful open mountain ranges with sunsets so picturesque that my photo album from the trip looks fake.

I didn't realize there would be ZERO service out there since it was only about thirty to forty minutes from civilization. But I had to find a way to check in. There were two options: dial-up Internet at the hunting lodge or one bar of phone service at the top of the mountains.

I would check my email in the morning and at night, and as we were stalking pigs, I would pause on mountaintops and see if I could reply to any of the board emails I was receiving. The result of the bickering was that no one could agree on a solution.

So, everyone agreed that they wanted to sell the business.

This didn't sit right with me. We were in the middle of the biggest boom in our company's history, with new products launching and innovation in the pipeline. It was also a very unstable time with COVID-19 and global economic uncertainty.

Standing on a mountaintop, holding my phone in the air to try to capture cell reception, it didn't feel like the right time to sell the business. I understood why everyone wanted to move in that direction. And maybe it was time. It had been thirteen years of getting the shit kicked out of me, and maybe it was time to listen to the elder statesmen. My rational brain said if we could sell the business for a large profit and make everyone happy that would be a good thing. And I would just figure out something else to do.

But my gut continued to say the timing was all wrong.

Still, the board went ahead to flesh out the idea of a sale. They selected three investment banking groups to evaluate us and went with a Major Bank. Major Bank gave us some monster valuation range and had just sold a direct competitor of ours for 200 million. Major Bank told the board everything they wanted to hear. I personally thought we should have gone with a boutique investment banking group that specialized in CPG brands. I love the underdog grinders who have something to prove. But the Graybeards in the room told me to take a seat and let the big dogs do what they do. So, we signed with Major Bank.

## For Sale?

The process began with three super nerds asking us questions about the business so they could begin putting together the prospectus to take out to potential acquirers. I'm no investment banking expert, but I kept asking myself: How in the hell are they going to be able to get someone excited about our brand? They can't even get excited about themselves, let alone a fucking salad dressing. There is just no way. But everyone reassured me that these guys knew what they were doing and that I should let them run their process.

Famous last fucking words.

I did it. I let them run their process. And we were supposed to start the bidding on Tessemae's in May.

Didn't happen. These fucking nerds seemed to need every piece of data under the sun before we launched. But in reality, the Major Bank was selling another dressing brand as well and had not told us. So Tessemae's was stuck with the "B Team," wasting time, spending money on irrelevant shit, and making this prospectus so fucking complicated that no one would be able to get excited about it even if they had taken four Viagra and an 8 ball of coke.

By July, Major Bank finally launched the bidding process. I'm not a rocket scientist, but the last time I checked, timing is everything, and rich people take vacations in the summer, so this seemed like the worst possible time to go to market. By August, everyone came back and said, "We really like the dressing business but hate the produce business." Major Bank suggested we split the companies in two and just sell the dressing business since the market placed zero value on the produce business. In my head, I was thinking: *If you guys could sell anything, this deal would be done by now. But sure, we will spend the next month jumping through 1,000 hoops because you suck at your job*. But everyone agreed that the dressing business was more marketable and that this would be a good thing long term.

After our Ironman race of hoop jumping, we went back out to the market with just the salad dressing company. Still crickets. This time, everyone just kind of stood around and made excuses as to why they weren't putting in a bid. I don't know what the Major Bank people were saying about us behind closed doors, but they were fucking it up. I had been turning down sale offers for five years, and to think we couldn't get anyone really excited about a brand with unlimited upside seemed fishy.

## Coach Fred on Offense

Coach Fred & Crew took that moment to completely flip the fuck out and direct all energy on removing me from the situation. "Greg broke his fiduciary duty by focusing on the produce business, and we want him and the management team out." That was the first communication from Coach Fred's team when Major Bank told them we didn't have any large bids.

I was shocked they chose me as the scapegoat. But then everyone piled on in some capacity. Henry was pissed because he wanted to sell it and it didn't. He took this moment to blame us for even being in this situation because of the Bald Barney Template. Now Henry officially hated both Coach Fred and Tessemae's. Coach Fred's team took the opportunity to not only cast doubt on the competence of the team but the board in general and attempted to take over the business. They lawyered up and began unleashing hell. They had the Bald Barney Template—a "signed document" that said they were getting 30 percent of the business and a total of two board seats, and they were going to get what was on the document.

Our lawyers stood strong and argued that the document was bogus and this was just a tactic to create chaos to get people on their side. But Coach Fred's team was going for broke. Coach Fred decided to try to buy Henry's board seat. Even though they hated each other, Coach Fred's team reached out to Henry directly and laid out a plan: Sell us your board seat, be done with this bullshit, let the professionals take over, and we both win. Henry was interested. If an enemy of your enemy is a friend—and everyone was Henry's enemy at this stage—anyone could be his friend. But there was only one problem with that deal coming to fruition: I had to approve it.

When we got word that Coach Fred was working directly with Henry there were some potential upsides. Coach Fred had no one to run the company, so if Henry did sell his seat then we would only be dealing with ONE psycho billionaire instead of two. That seemed refreshing. But more so, Coach Fred would actually be vested in the deal because his debt would officially be equity. It wasn't a wonderful situation, to say the least, but we were looking for some Sun Tzu's *The Art of War* shit to make this battle digestible.

But God works in mysterious ways, and the beautiful old saying, "Pigs get fat, hogs get slaughtered" rang true. Initially, the board and our lawyers said this could be a good thing. If Coach Fred would just slide into Henry's spot, we keep the board at three, and everything would stay the same. We could manage the board's rights as our negotiating points, and everyone would win. So, we began the process of negotiating the terms of the buyout of Henry's board seat.

It initially looked like it was going to get done relatively easily, but Coach Fred is a hog, not a pig, and couldn't be satisfied with a GOOD deal. He wanted a GREAT one. So, he called and wanted a better deal. He wanted us to honor the outrageous bullshit that was in the Bald Barney Template: 30 percent equity and buy the additional board seat. The three million dollars promised in the Bald Barney Template and Henry's board seat were two completely different deals. But they wanted to leverage the emotion of one to get the benefit of the other—classic hogs.

Our main focus continued to be Henry's board seat. Henry's rights were legitimately a concern to the well-being of the other shareholders if Coach Fred took over. The problem with Henry's board seat was that his rights trumped everyone else's votes as the final say. So, if Coach Fred bought the board seat without us changing Henry's existing power, Coach Fred could basically make any decision he wanted. Coach Fred's team continued to focus on the three million dollars. But all the voting power was in the board seat, not the three million. So that had me wondering: Why were they harping on the three million dollars so intently? They kept saying the deals HAD TO BE DONE TOGETHER, or they wouldn't do them at all.

But the more we dug into the three million in template money, the less we liked it. There were too many legal land mines and conspiracy theories tied to this money, and we needed clarity. We needed to start testing whether or not these dudes were acting in bad faith.

## The Workflow Hypothesis

I wrote out a workflow of decisions that would tell us where Coach Fred's team stood.

The first way to test their intentions was to focus on the interest on their money and the conversion of all their money to equity. They had been screaming the entire time they wanted their money back, but in the deal structure that Bald Barney sent over, he had a portion of the money remaining as debt and the interest continuing to accrue. Why? Why wouldn't they make the interest payable and just take a lump sum chunk of cash that was owed to them? I mean, billionaires were making this massive stink over three million bucks, even though their interest that could be paid was over four million. It seemed like a simple negotiating point, but it had major consequences.

Brendan the SEAL had a crazy conspiracy theory about the accruing interest: They wanted it to accrue because there was no time limit on when it had to be converted to equity. In theory, they could buy Henry's board seat, cancel raising money, and just let the debt continue to accrue interest at the predetermined valuation number and just own 100 percent of the company without having to do anything.

It didn't sound crazy to me. It sounded like Coach Fred's next move.

The fact that we were negotiating a deal that was going to strip away the financial upside from our existing investors, all over this minuscule three million dollars was insane. If we went through with it, we would be in court for the next 100 years. So, we needed clarity: Was Coach Fred acting in good faith or not? If Coach Fred & Crew accepted our arrangement that allowed the interest to be paid instead of accruing, they were acting in good faith. If they continued to focus on the interest accruing and not budge on that deal point, Brendan the SEAL's "crazy" conspiracy theory was true.

Another test: If we said no to including the renegotiation of the three million dollars in this board seat deal, then per their nonstop bitching, the deal would be dead in the water. If they moved forward with Henry's board seat after we called their "dead in the water bluff" on the three million dollars, then we know exactly what they were up to; Coach Fred & Crew wanted the entire company.

In my gut, I knew they wanted the company. But I prayed they were good people. Because if they were in fact acting in bad faith, and ALL THESE THINGS HAPPENED, I would have to unleash a legal nuclear war.

I wrote out my Good Faith vs Bad Faith workflow and sent it to Brendan the SEAL and our outside counsel. The plan was to see if I was right on the full scope of bad faith by actually negotiating the sale of the board seat AND the three million dollars. That way, we could finally confirm what I already knew in my gut about Coach Fred & Crew. If I was wrong and viewed as a conspiracy theorist, great. The company would be in a good spot, and I look like a dumbass. But if I was right, and all this insane "crazy" bullshit was true, we dodged a hostile takeover. Seemed like a win-win.

So, the board seat negotiation began, and the initial conversations with Bald Barney and Brendan the SEAL were good. Everything was via email with lawyers copied, and things were moving right along—except for the issue of the interest accruing. We would send our deal points over indicating the interest was paid, they would email back indicating the interest accruing. Every other deal point had been agreed upon except for the interest. "This isn't good," I thought.

Then I heard from Coach Fred's team. I tried to have a conversation with them, but all they kept doing was repeating the same phrase over and over, using the industry term for changing a deal after the handshake: *You re-traded our deal, Greg. Why did you re-trade our deal, Greg?*

It was like negotiating with robots.

I finally told them: "Unless you have anything else to say outside of the words 're-trading the deal,' this call is done. You have our final offer. Take it or leave it." And I hung up. I called the board and told them they were not going to budge from the Bald Barney Template deal. They want that interest accruing, and they made that very clear. Everyone agreed it was time to walk away from their deal entirely.

I wrote a long letter to Coach Fred walking away from renegotiating the three million as a part of the Henry's Board seat sale:

Dear Fred,

I had hoped we would be in a different place by now. I truly feel that we were brought together for a reason. Our relationship has ebbed and flowed but I always had an underlying hope that you would grow into the mentor that I never had.

"You don't rise to your expectations, you fall back to your training." And I think that's where we are right now.

You have a group of professional investors that want more and always will, it's their training. I see 53 investors that have gotten us here at different stages of this journey, with each stage being a different level of my training as a CEO. Regardless of their feelings toward me, or my feelings in general, I have a responsibility to everyone.

My North Star has always been to trust my gut. And my gut is telling me that your group no longer has trust in me. It's unfortunate because I have always tried to be a straight shooter. My candor and willingness to trust has hurt me during my life and it appears this is one of those times. You asked me to call you with the plan after our original phone call regarding this deal and I did that. There was a miscommunication, and you were then "benched." I tried to have a similar relationship with your partners and they told me to "let the lawyers do their jobs and stay out of it." When I took that advice and let the lawyers do their jobs, I was told I somehow re-traded this deal. Regardless of your feelings on that point, that was never my intent. My assumption was always that you and I could work things out because of our mutual respect and trust for each other but I think we can both agree that's not there anymore.

My main focus has always been and will always be to build Tessemae's into a great American consumer packaged goods brand. That objective requires complete heart and focus, all of which I have not had, due to the distraction of this attempted transaction, and the distraction of the events this past Fall. I will not continue that pattern. It is my responsibility to every investor to focus on the task at hand and ensure I work towards a positive outcome for everyone. We are close to a transformational event through our process with a major bank, and I cannot and will not trip at the goal line due to a lack of focus.

My job is still to build and lead this brand and to protect all the people who have helped me along the way, including you. Every journey has a beginning and an end. I didn't think we were at the end point of our relationship but maybe we are.

At the beginning of this process several weeks ago, I was told that if we changed one comma of the deal, the deal was off. I think that it has unfortunately taken us several weeks and six figures of legal bills to realize that trading favors so that we can avoid a problem today only sets us up for more problems tomorrow. This deal has evolved into something that concerns me on every level, and I believe it is simply not a good idea. Not for you, not for us, not for anyone. I have been running this company for 12 years and counting, and I am still alive. I will find a solution to our current problems and I will find a way to win for us all.

I honestly don't know if you are relieved to be off the hook, or angry. Of course, I hope it is the former. For all you have done for me and the company this far, I will get you the outcome that you want, even if it means we simply part ways. In the meantime, I think it's best if I get back to coaching the team.

Sincerely, Greg

Coach Fred immediately tried calling to get me back on his side, but I didn't pick up. I said what I needed to say and was tired of being lied to, like a five-star high school quarterback being recruited to a top university. After I didn't pick up Coach Fred's call, his team wrote an email saying they were still going to move forward with buying Henry's board seat with or without the three million being renegotiated. The bad faith workflow "test" I wrote out was unfolding just as I imagined. I learned that night that Coach Fred had reached out to Henry directly, and they were going to find a way to take over the company together.

The only thing left for me to do. I needed to hit the nuclear button.

## Field Guide: Lessons Learned

### What You Need to Know
Only YOU can sell the passion.

### How to Do It
People will say trust the experts. Don't believe them. Insert yourself and make the "experts" prove their worth to you. Set clear and unemotional metrics for the "experts" to hit and be ruthless with your expectations. In the moment it will feel like you are micromanaging the situation or stepping on peoples toes. It will feel like you are not the expert randomly trying to take the lead on a project you know nothing about. Trust me when I say this, the passion and authenticity that you will bring to any meeting is worth more than any data point an "expert" may bring. People are numb to the "sales guy" bullshit. They want to know what they are buying and why. You are the reason.

### What You Need to Know
You are only good to them when you are hitting home runs.

### How to Do It
Reframe your mind to what your job actually is. It doesn't matter if you started it. It doesn't matter if you are the face of it. Your investors and stakeholders only want home runs. Your job is to hit home runs and make sure everyone else is hitting home runs as well. If you are only hitting singles, they are going to become antsy and look to replace you.

### What You Need to Know
Loop in people to your gut.

### How to Do It
Your job is to read between the lines and connect the dots. Sometimes you need more dots to connect, and that's when you need to loop people in. I kept five or six people around me who always had their ears to the ground. I could call and tell them my gut feelings. Those calls would then plant seeds in their radars to keep a lookout. More often than not, I was right, and it allowed us to fight another day. Your gut intuition is always trying to tell you something. Figure out how to translate the code.

# SIXTEEN

Home Office Henry and Coach Fred & Crew were now working directly with each other.

There was still some hope among the management team that they wouldn't go forward with the sale of Henry's board seat to Coach Fred, but I knew it would happen. They had a mutual enemy now in me and Tessemae's. Combining forces almost guaranteed all their goals would be met: greed, ego, and power. Combining forces also allowed the Baltimore power hierarchy to remain organized the way Henry liked it—with him at the top of the org chart.

Our lawyer said that I could still block the transaction if I was willing to unleash hell and start World War III. I obviously didn't want to battle two billionaires at once. I wasn't just fighting for my livelihood, I also represented the rest of the fifty shareholders. *Fortitudine Vincimus* is a quote I have painted in my gym . . . *Through endurance, we conquer.* I can grind forever, and I'm not sure my opponents wanted to. Yes, they had more money than I did, but I was pretty sure of one thing: If they decided to take me down, it was going to take a lot of money, time, and stress on their part to pull it off. The man in the mirror does not lie, and at some point, you are going to have to brush your teeth.

## Board Battles, Take One

Unsurprisingly, Coach Fred decided to go "all in" after Henry's seat. He began making up shit about me to get Henry on his side. Brendan the SEAL, still getting weekly tongue lashings from his former employer, Henry, confirmed what I was hearing: Coach Fred was going to own this company and destroy me or die in the process.

And I mean that literally.

Coach Fred's health was horrible. He had a host of serious health problems. But watching him come for me explained a lot of those health woes. I watched him sacrifice everything he said he stood for in the pursuit of greed, ego, power, and revenge. To witness the transformation of someone who claimed to be a man of "God and character" into the living embodiment of several of the seven deadly sins was quite a scene. It was Dr. Jekyll and Mr. Hyde to the max. And I can attest to deadly sins being deadly because, with each passing day, Coach Fred's health would get worse and worse. His true colors were shown, and I didn't need any more evidence to understand what kind of man he was.

Just as I predicted, Coach Fred offered Henry a deal he couldn't refuse: Eleven million for the board seat. It seemed like a high price to pay for a board seat, but if you have revenge on the mind, you aren't thinking rationally.

The paperwork was sent over to the board to approve, and it was the moment of truth: hand over the company to Coach Fred or block the sale of the board seat. There were a lot of potential implications of blocking the sale of the board seat. The lawsuits, the slander, the loss of investor prestige in the Baltimore community, the access that these people would have, and the cost to defend the decision in court. I considered giving up. But then I thought about the other fifty investors and the money they put in. I thought about writing a story of my life and that sale being the final chapter in the

Book of Tessemae's. I thought about how much time and energy had gone into trying to do what was right all those years and the sacrifices made. To give it to Coach Fred? Was that how I was willing to go out? Was this the best thing for the other shareholders? Was this how the story ended?

The voice in my head said no. *Fuck this. I ain't goin' out like this. I'll fight to the death, and we'll see who is left standing.* I decided to block the sale of the seat and take my chances. We sent word back to Coach Fred's legal team that the sale was not going to go through because it would negatively affect the company and other shareholders. Henry went fucking berserk. We had just "taken" eleven million out of his pocket, and in his eyes, this little salad-dressing hustling peasant just stole it from him.

He lawyered up with the best and the brightest and unleashed them on our lawyers. But they found nothing. The biggest issue for Henry was the strong possibility that if he went through selling his board seat and Coach Fred went through what we thought his plan was, Henry could be in court for the next decade facing investor backlash and breach of fiduciary duty as a board member. That didn't stop Henry from spending cash on lawyers to pressure test our resolve.

Once the initial onslaught of legal bombings happened, Henry moved on to his next prey, and the bombings died down. However, his lawyers stayed close to Coach Fred's team, and they continued to plot our downfall. With Coach Fred's newfound rage over not being able to buy the board, his legal team didn't sleep. There was a new accusation or legal theory almost daily. But none of them worked, which pissed him off even more. How in the fuck could our simple salad-dressing asses be outmaneuvering his world-class team? He had the "best," and we were a bunch of *Bad News Bears*. But Coach Fred was on a mission and would not be denied come hell or high water.

In Coach Fred's emotional rage, his legal team made a critical error: they filed a suit in court claiming Breach of Contract. Now our fight was public. When Ryan, our loan sharkish lender, saw this, his company reengaged with vengeance. Ryan the Shark and his group smelled blood and knew that because all the major investors were in turmoil. They realized they could cause more chaos while we were distracted and weak.

## Supply Chain Woes

And then, just when you think you've seen it all, the global supply chain crisis hits us. The only thing we were missing from our downpour of plagues were locusts. Letters started coming in from our suppliers that read: "Regardless of previously contracted pricing, we will be passing through any changes in price due to the unstable global economic outlook."

Excuse me?

We called all of our retailers and all of our buyers—they confirmed that they would accept the pass through of price changes. All except the Big Box Retailer. They knew the supply chain crisis was happening. They just didn't know how long it was going to last. So, they hedged that it was going to pass quickly. If they didn't change their prices and stalled their suppliers by suggesting they would eventually get around to it, the Big Box Retailer would continue to have low prices—and competitive advantage in the marketplace where competitor prices were rising.

This created a significant squeeze for Tessemae's. The Big Box Retailer prices weren't changing, and the produce side of our business started to become a problem. A thirty-six million business unit that was once printing money was now losing money. We were calling the Big Box HQ daily about the pricing changes but there was no movement.

This added a completely new dynamic to the investor predicament we were in because now the threat of bankruptcy was becoming more real by the second. We had multiple lawsuits going on at once, costing $300,000 a month in legal fees. The retail landscape was unstable and unpredictable, and now our predictable and steady produce business was sucking away all our cash and distracting everyone on the team to try to solve that problem.

Partner Paul from our board suggested we "get ahead of it" and hired a professional negotiator who specializes in restructuring. If we could solve some of the problems we were dealing with and reduce our monthly exposure, then there was a chance we could survive this moment. He connected us with Nicky, who had worked with Partner Paul's son on restructuring negotiations.

Now Nicky was used to negotiating this kind of deal on a much larger scale, so he came in with the attitude that our negotiation would be a cakewalk. To him, we were just a little salad dressing company with little problems. He interviewed everyone to try to get a deeper understanding of what he was walking into, and in his mind, it seemed very cut and dry. I tried to warn him about the irrational nature of the people we were dealing with. I told him: "These dudes don't want to compromise; they only want one thing, and that is 'everything.' Unless you are giving them that, they ain't budging." Negotiator Nicky chuckled and told me: "Everybody acts that way until the rubber meets the road."

I didn't chuckle. I just said, "I hope you're right."

Nicky had his work cut out for him. And I knew he didn't believe me when I told him what was coming.

## Salad Standoff

Negotiator Nicky had a full plate: In addition to trying to negotiate with Coach Fred, Henry, and Ryan the Shark, he added on discussions with our farming partners regarding the PACA debt we were racking up due to the change in commodity prices. We had tried for weeks to work with the Big Box Retailer about the pricing changes on our salads, and they just kept saying they would get around to it. After Nicky spoke to the farmers and realized how severe the situation was regarding the PACA liability, he told the board we needed to get rid of the produce business immediately. It was draining all of our resources and racking up a potentially catastrophic debt that we had no way of paying back. But who was going to buy a produce business that was losing money in the middle of a supply chain crisis? The answer was: only an idiot. And we didn't have one handy.

We went to Big Box one last time and pleaded our case for pricing changes on the salads, and again they figured we were bluffing. But this time, instead of ending the call with our heads hanging low from another unproductive call, we let them know how serious it was. "We will no longer be shipping salads to you until the prices change. We are already losing money on every salad, and that stops today."

The Big Box Retailer probably thought we were playing a game of chicken with them, and we would bail at the last second, but after one week went by and we had shipped nothing, they knew we were serious. Then two weeks went by, and zero salads shipped. By week three, the Big Box HQ called an emergency meeting with us "to figure this out." There wasn't much to figure out: We told them the same thing that we had been telling them—change your prices or we are not shipping. They agreed to do it but said it would take awhile to get changes through their system. We told them: "When it changes in your system, is when we'll ship you salads again, but not before that."

Everyone on the board was now freaking the fuck out. The PACA debt was its own looming crisis, and the only way to fix it was to pay off the four million or get rid of Tessemae's produce business. We were still paying rent, payroll, and utilities, and yet finding a solution for the produce business had become everyone's main focus. The board suggested we sell the produce business to our California lettuce partners since their pricing had changed. I explained to the board that our lettuce partner was getting fucking demolished from the COVID-19 supply chain one-two punch. They weren't going to want to buy our business. But the board was convinced they would.

So, we presented our California lettuce partners with the deal to buy the produce business from Tessemae's: Assume the PACA debt, take over the expenses, and give us some cash for the contracts, and it's yours. It was a bizarrely fair deal, but they were losing ungodly amounts of money at the time.

They countered with: they would take the contracts, not the debt, and no cash. So, we would basically be paying them four million dollars to take the produce business off our hands. I've seen some dumb deals in my life but this could have been the dumbest. We respectfully declined.

Now that the California lettuce partners weren't an option, discussions around just shutting the doors and walking away started to bubble up. "We can't keep carrying these expenses and losing money, just shut the doors!" Negotiator Nicky said. I reminded everyone that those farmers would be coming after that four million through the PACA trust and Tessemae's didn't have it. And since Tessemae's didn't have it, they were coming after the board for the money.

The board started screaming like it was the end of the world because the PACA risk was now very personal for them. It came to a head when I had to take a board conference call while sitting in a parking lot about to coach my daughter's lacrosse practice, and after about ten minutes of nonsense, I screamed, "Just shut the fuck up. I'll fucking buy it. I'll assume all the debt from Tessemae's, take over the payroll immediately, and set up a supply contract with Tessemae's that locks in the price of the salad dressing pouches for the next decade so the margins are strong. That way we can keep the 1.5-oz pouch revenue coming into Tessemae's, and all of our risk leaves the dressing business so we can sell it."

Everyone paused.

They asked me to get off the call, so they could discuss it without me and would call me back.

Twenty minutes later, they called and said it was mine. They would write up the sales agreement and get it over to me.

I called my brothers and explained what I had just done. "Well, boys, we better be able to renegotiate these contracts with the Big Box Retailer or we are all going bankrupt."

## The Birth of Alta

I got more details the next day: I was to put in 1.5 million dollars to stabilize the raw materials, assume the 4.5 million of debt, and take over the payroll and operating expenses immediately to make it a done deal.

I called Brian and told him to set up a meeting with the Big Box Retailer that day. We got on the call, and I explained the full situation: "If you want us to risk everything we have on you and these salads, I need you to extend the contracts on these salads with the new pricing for one year. We are not going to lose our homes and ruin our kids' lives for you to give the contracts to someone else in sixty days." The VP of produce paused. He spoke to his counterpart and replied, "You have one year, and that's all I will commit to. The rest is up to you guys. But if you all mess this up, I'm giving the contracts to someone else."

We told them messing up was not an option for us; we'd be perfect.

Brian and I refinanced our homes for the 1.5 million and set up Alta as a new company.

Now that the PACA debt was off the board's shoulders and solely on mine (which didn't seem to bother them at all), we got back to finding some agreement with Coach Fred, Henry, and Ryan the Shark. Nicky continued to have calls with their respective legal teams with zero progress. His frustration levels began to resemble ours. A familiar look of rage and exhaustion covered his face every time we jumped on a Zoom call. He wasn't making any progress whatsoever, and it almost felt like things were getting worse.

Then we received a note that Henry was pulling his lieutenant off the board, but reserving all the rights and powers of the seat.

What the fuck did that mean? He was removing the oars from the row boat. How the fuck were we going to be able to vote on matters without the third guy to vote. We decided that was exactly Henry's plan. And the moral of that story is: take eleven million dollars from a billionaire with a big ego, and he will find a way to fuck you.

## Board Battle, Take Two

Our lawyer looked through our operating agreement and found a clause that allowed us to keep things moving forward as long as we made every attempt possible to get the votes from the third board seat in a timely manner. With the stakes rising, all the pressure fell on board member Partner Paul. He was the only independent board member left for Coach Fred and Ryan the Shark's group to lean on, and they knew it. When word got out that Henry had "removed the oars from the rowboat" everyone started calling Paul. Not only was that too much work and time for Paul, but the amount of risk he was assuming was increasing by the day. He then made a strategic decision to execute what our lawyers explained was "an action causing event" by stepping down from the board to try to force everyone to the negotiating table.

That left me as the sole board member with all liability on me and me alone. Not only had I just put all the PACA debt on my family and my brother's family, but now I had all the Tessemae's liability as well.

Partner Paul and Nicky remained present, as counselors and advisors. But the buck stopped with me. Partner Paul's action causing event did, in fact, spook Coach Fred & Crew. When word got to them about Henry's board seat, Coach Fred & Crew immediately called Partner Paul and began negotiating a deal. Paul had always been the last stop on the train when it came to people peppering the board with bullshit. And it usually never made it to him. He would hear our stories and comment, but he was rarely running point on the nonsense. That all changed with Paul's action causing event.

For about six weeks, Coach Fred & Crew went back and forth discussing a path forward together with Partner Paul. Coach Fred & Crew have a long-running strategy for deals, which involves endless discussions around simple topics, with multiple people calling you about different topics to confuse and fatigue you. They each play a role: Coach Fred is the "head coach, atta boy" guy. Fred's First Lieutenant is the reasonable elder statesman who appeals to your rational side. Fred's Second Lieutenant is the unemotional entrepreneur who shares his war stories with you to try to build rapport.

Partner Paul was getting this encirclement nonstop. After six weeks, he called me and said, "We have a deal done, and it's fair but not great. They are going to send over the final outline shortly so we can all review it." I asked what the 30,000-foot view was, and he outlined it. "Coach Fred's team takes over the operations and the existing Tessemae's team runs the sales, marketing, and branding. The board would be redone, and we would look to sell it within two years. The Vetters would be 'on contract' for one year, and then they want to get rid of you as soon as they can, but you would keep your equity in the business."

I paused and thought: *This was a reasonable way to die.* I processed it all for a couple of days and didn't see a better option. Brendan the SEAL asked me to call Coach Fred and resolve our differences before signing the deal because Coach Fred was in the hospital and might not make it. I did not want to make the call at all. The phrase "eating a frog" didn't explain how much shit I had to eat to make the call.

My thought was this: If Coach Fred dies today, would I regret not making the call because I was being a coward?

I called Coach Fred's number, and he picked up. "Greg? Is that you?"

Jokingly I said, "What the hell are you doing laying down in a hospital bed for? We got shit to do!"

He chuckled, and we talked about how Tessemae's needs to stop fighting and start winning, which I agreed with. He said, "I don't want to talk about the past at all. Let's just start fresh and focus on the future." I agreed and told him to get better.

I let Brendan the SEAL know I made the call, and he thanked me for doing so. For the rest of the day, I felt like a weight had been lifted off my shoulder. I took the high road, and it felt good. One enemy down, two to go. Things were looking up. The next day, Coach Fred's team sent over the deal from Partner Paul's six-week negotiation.

And it was nothing Partner Paul said it was. It was completely different per fucking usual. Nothing they'd agreed to was in the deal. Instead, it was Coach Fred's team taking over 100 percent of the business and firing the Vetters on Day One. It was a good old-fashioned public square beheading.

Paul was in shock. "How could they change these things like this?! I have spent six fucking weeks talking to these crooked bastards. This is unbelievable! I am fucking speechless!"

So, it wasn't one enemy down. Taking the high road apparently did nothing except give me the temporary and false sensation of hope.

We all lawyered up again and went right back into the shit.

## Courtroom Clash

As the Coach Fred drama was unfolding, we had another hearing regarding Ryan the Shark's group. They had changed their lawyers three separate times and changed their lawsuit more than that. This hearing centered around our "default" again. And was scheduled for Monday morning at nine a.m. On Sunday evening at five p.m., Ryan's group finally added their actual complaint. It stated that they were unaware that we were raising money to pay them off. And per the loan documents, we had to notify them of any additional funds being raised.

Our lawyers walked in to the courtroom the next day and asked for two weeks to prepare our defense since the timing of the complaint was outrageous. Over the next two weeks, our team put together forty-five pages of emails, text messages, calendar invites, sworn affidavits, and testimonials explaining how Ryan's group knew about us raising money. We'd seen the group submitting sworn affidavits and testimonies that we knew were lies. We went into court assuming they were going to go to jail for perjury.

The hearing was supposed to be less than an hour because of all the evidence submitted ahead of time, but as the hearing unfolded, the judge didn't seem to care about our evidence at all. It was as if we didn't submit anything. The judge just started asking questions of Ryan's group, as if we were lying. Our lawyer was in such shock he literally interrupted the judge and said, "I'm sorry but I'm not sure what is going on here. You asked us to provide evidence that they knew about us raising money, which we have in great detail. Yet you are ignoring all of it and acting like it's made up. I'm completely in shock as to what is happening right now."

After four hours of this, the judge said he needed to review the information in more detail and get back to us. This was not good. This was supposed to be simple. We were sure we had a slam dunk.

If the judge somehow sided with Ryan's group, we would owe them fifteen million, and if we appealed, the appeal bond was 15 percent of that figure.

What in the actual fuck was going on?

I called Partner Paul the next day to explain what had happened in the courtroom, and he agreed this was very bad news. We only had one option left: press the nuclear button.

---

## Field Guide: Lessons Learned

### What You Need to Know
Just do what is right.

### How to Do It
There will be moments when you can line your pockets and fuck someone over . . . everyone has those moments. And in that moment, imagine this is the movie of your life, and everyone you have ever cared about is going to watch the film. How do you want them to react during that scene? How will you feel in the movie theater sitting next to them? Make the decision with that in mind.

### What You Need to Know
Every action has a greater reaction.

### How to Do It
Take that equation to heart when you are making decisions. We live in a time where character and honor are as rare as the Ferrari in *Ferris Bueller's Day Off*. People are sharks these days. You can no longer assume that people will do what is right or what is expected. What is twice the reaction to the decision you are about to make? What does a three-times reaction look like?

Write it down and think on it. This extra moment of reflection will allow you to frame your decisions properly.

**What You Need to Know**

Watch out for the scorpion.

**How to Do It**

Maybe you've heard this fable: Once upon a time, there was a scorpion who wanted to get across a river but could not swim. So, he asked a frog to carry him. The frog wasn't so sure, concerned the scorpion would sting him. The scorpion promised not to, and pointed out that it would be stupid to kill his ride—then they'd both die. The frog decided this was sensible and agreed. Halfway across, the scorpion stung the frog. As they both sank, the frog asked the scorpion why he did that—dooming them both. The scorpion replied that he couldn't help it; it was his nature. The moral of this story: Once you identify the scorpion, keep them away. It doesn't matter if the scorpions say they have changed. They have not. Behavior is consistent and always will be. Talk is cheap, and scorpions kill. Just remember that.

# Epilogue

The nuclear button.

The thing I avoided at all costs for my entire journey.

The scarlet letter.

The confirmation of every hater.

The ultimate measure of failure in my eyes.

Bankruptcy.

Now, in legal terms, we were talking about Chapter 11, not Chapter 7. Chapter 11 is a reorganization. Chapter 7 is a liquidation. There's a big difference in business circles. But to the common man, it's exactly the same.

We had no other option. No one would negotiate with us and now that there was a chance that our lender could lie their way into fifteen million bucks. We had to press pause and go back to the drawing board. We knew we couldn't spend two million on the appeal bond only to continue to have Ryan the Shark's group lie in court. Our only option for the safety of everyone was Chapter 11.

What did that even mean? What did this mean for me? What did this mean for my family? What did this mean for the business? I literally knew nothing on this subject—by design. And why should I? I had avoided even speaking the word "bankruptcy" for the past fifteen years.

As we hired our lawyers and began mapping out the Chapter 11 process, I couldn't help but feel like the biggest piece of shit that had ever lived. I looked back on my life and, specifically, Tessemae's journey and thought about every person who had ever told me I was going to be a failure. I could still see their faces and hear their voices. It was those moments that had inspired me. I tried as hard as I could to prove them wrong. So hard, that I made it true.

The Oscar Wilde quote rang in my head: "Each man kills the thing he loves." Is that what I did? Did I white knuckle grip this thing so hard that I choked it to death? Did I force my way in, keeping this business working for so long when it should have died years ago?

I called my buddy, who is a hedge fund manager and self-made billionaire, to gain a little perspective. He specializes in merging companies and winding them down, and I needed some "varsity insight" and not just the bullshit going through my head.

"Hey, man, I need your insight. We're going to be filing Chapter 11 next week, and I'm trying to process it in my head. I feel like a total fucking failure, and I need your insight on Chapter 11 and how I should be thinking about it."

He responded, "Greggy, this shit happens every day. You tried to negotiate with everyone and they wouldn't. You have been spending all your money and time on bringing these people to the table and they won't. And now it's time. This is called a strategic reorganization. I know this has been your baby, and you're emotional about the journey, but for us veterans in the business game, we do this shit all the time. This was strategic. You can't be thinking small."

I laughed and said, "The next time I see you, and you call me *Greggy*, I am going to bear hug you until your ribs break." I also thanked him for his guidance and insight in my time of need.

I appreciated his perspective, but it didn't make the roller coaster I was on any less stomach churning. Before we could even file for Chapter 11, we had to get every investor's sign-off. The lawyers sent out an update to investors, asking for their signatures approving the process. Ten out of the fifty took this moment to unleash hell on me and Tessemae's. I could have predicted that reaction from that particular ten, but it didn't make it any easier to have their disdain delivered to me in writing.

After our lawyers spoke to them, they signed the approval to file, and the paperwork was submitted on a Friday afternoon. All weekend, I sat and reflected on fifteen years of blood, sweat, and tears and attempted to process this being one of the last chapters in the book of my journey. There was still a chance that a miracle could happen, but this time, instead of attempting to bend the universe to my will, I wanted to see where this road was going to take me. I had been trying to control everything up to that point, and it had gotten me here, so maybe it was time to let go and see where the white water would carry me. I had a new perspective on the Chapter 11 process, which made it a little easier to digest, but the scarlet letter branded into my chest still hurt.

Joseph Campbell has a wonderful quote that always proves true in my experience: "The cave you fear to enter holds the treasures you seek." My cave had always been bankruptcy. When we filed, there was an initial phase of complete and utter chaos—people calling and emailing and trying to get around the system. Exactly what I had always feared. But then . . . all the madness stopped. There was quiet. Everyone had to go through the bankruptcy attorneys and follow the process. All the lawsuits paused. All the debt payments paused. The only thing we could do was make salad dressing and ship it. The treasure.

Now there were good things that were paused as well—people's compensation, money owed to employees and vendors. So, everyone was still pissed. But I still felt it: to be able to just make salad dressing without insane lawsuits and investor coups was cool to experience again. We hadn't done that since 2017. That's how long we had been fighting off takeover attempts. That's how long I had been avoiding the cave.

The team was reduced to four full-time employees and two part-time contractors. We moved all the manufacturing to West Virginia and shut down our plant in Baltimore. My brothers, Kristen, and Moe moved over to Alta to run and scale that business, and Tessemae's went through the Chapter 11 process.

Now, to say it was "refreshing" would be an inaccurate way to describe the bankruptcy process, but watching people forced to present their case to a judge who had the authority to make the final decision once and for all was beautiful to see. All the bullshit, all the backstabbing, all the fear, paused.

Ryan's group, true to form, decided to remain our enemy. But everyone else put their weapons down and joined our side to try to get a good outcome for everyone. Everything wasn't rainbows and sunshine. People were still fucking pissed, and all the lawyers agreed the only way to get everyone to stop dragging their feet was to sell Tessemae's through the Chapter 11 bankruptcy called a 363 Sale. It was time. I was finally ready to let Tessemae's go. We created a company, grew it to be valued at over 300 million dollars, and sold it out at a bankruptcy auction for 4.5 million.

I probably should have sold it multiple times during the journey—taken the money and ran. But in retrospect, I am glad I didn't. I needed to understand the true and unfiltered journey of a bootstrapped entrepreneur's dream. All the bad, all the good, all the shit, all the backstabbings. All the lost allies, confidants, friends, and foes. But also, what it takes to stand strong in the middle of the storm. I needed the full picture.

I remember in 2016 when a private equity group wanted to take us over and asked why I had not signed with them yet. I replied, "Because you will make me a figurehead, and I will not learn the playbook for myself. I want to know how this process works. I want to truly build something."

They looked at me and shook their heads. They knew what I was in for and what I was actually requesting for the rest of my journey. But I did want all of that. Give a man a fish or teach him to fish? Which would you choose? Hercules faced an epic decision at the crossroads: take the easy way and have everything you have ever wanted for the rest of your life and never lift a finger, OR be tested with the twelve labors to see what type of man you actually are. He chose the twelve labors and lived. I'm not sure what labor I am on out of the twelve, but this fight was a doozy.

As each day passed with the bankruptcy process, everyone became more distant. It was everyone for themselves and everyone watching their ass. I was surprised by this because we had always been a team. Everyone knew my family had sacrificed everything we owned to keep the company alive, but the moment things went into Chapter 11, Partner Paul retreated to his camp, Brendan the SEAL went to his, and our inside counsel worked directly with the lawyers and stopped talking to me for the most part. I tried to have our head of operations move to one of the companies I had started, but she grew distant with each passing day and eventually stopped talking to everyone altogether. And just like that, just like it had started, there was only me. Alone in a grocery store handing out samples with the hope of something better. Alone trying to convince my brothers to make salad dressing with me in the middle of the night at a rib restaurant.

Life cycles are just that, cycles. Humans are born needing support to live, and we die almost requiring the same amount of support. Tessemae's was no different. It would live or die with me. And just like death, I had no idea about what was next. Was it a new life cycle all over again? Was it the end of my life cycle in business and I would be reborn as something completely different? My journey thus far taught me it was time to let go and let the white water take me where it wanted to take me, and I was ready.

I said my goodbyes and moved on to mitigate any additional pain or risk. The Alta business flourished. We did exactly what we said we were going to do and turned it into a well-oiled machine that never misses an order and produces money hand over fist. Things tend to be way easier when you aren't fighting lawsuits and investor coups.

Before the bankruptcy, my brothers and I purchased 50 percent of the West Virginia co-packer that makes all of Tessemae's salad dressing. They were going to sell to a private equity group that would have prevented Tessemae's from surviving. So, I told them I would buy half of them, and there wouldn't be any bullshit.

That business continued to thrive and has doubled since we partnered. Everything I ever did was to make Tessemae's the next great American brand, but it felt forced. America doesn't care about clean salad dressing. Investors don't really care about how the sausage is made just as long as you give them a return. Most people don't have long-term vision and just want everything now. But in trying to save one thing, I found many others. I reaffirmed the fact that I do know what I am doing in business, regardless of what the haters tell me. I stopped forcing things and allowed the universe to flow to me if it so chooses. I found peace.

One of my great worries was that I was going to be a one-hit wonder. Tessemae's and then nothing—just a series of attempts to recreate the thing that, at one point, had so much buzz. I also worried that Tessemae's was the only thing keeping the Vetter brothers in business together, and that without a win, we would all go our separate ways. But that couldn't be farther from the truth. We continued together in multiple businesses, including Homegrown Brands, a brand accelerator that helps brands scale and avoid the bullshit we had to deal with. We have launched a half dozen businesses through that platform and they are all thriving regardless of what the haters had to say about our "track record." And in helping others, I realized I had manufactured the buzz and forced the brand. I had created the playbook that I had so longed to learn about, and now it could be applied to anything. And my brothers and I only do things now that make us smile.

I thought success was going to be a giant exit—a celebration of people looking from the outside in and celebrating me at some food show as the guy who made it. But it turned out that's not success at all. Success was understanding and appreciating the four things money can't buy: your health, your soul, your time, and your children's love. With each epic failure and obstacle overcome, I learned a little bit more about the meaning of success. I realized I had the playbook all along. This journey was just a way for me to understand the answers were always within. And success can be financial, but that's not the whole picture. Success has to be a part of a larger puzzle. It has to be a part of something worth fighting for. Money can't be the only thing. Recognition from strangers can't be part of the equation. The American Dream is having an idea and following it through, but it has to be done with a greater purpose: To lead by example, to make your kids proud, to keep your soul intact, to be loved by the people you care about, to continue to create and leave things better than when you found them.

When I lay my head down at night, I am proud of the man I am and the story I have lived. I am proud of the lessons I learned and what I can teach my kids. I am happy to teach other entrepreneurs what to avoid and what to look forward to. My journey was the same journey that Santiago had in *The Alchemist*. He had to go to the pyramids and nearly die to understand the treasure was beneath the tree he slept under every night prior to setting off on a journey of a lifetime. But he would not have believed it unless he lived the journey. And that's what I did. I lived the American Dream to its fullest. And it didn't end as I thought it would. It ended better. I went out like a

Viking on a funeral pyre fit for a battle-scarred warrior. But unlike the Viking, I got to live to fight another day. And I am proud of that.

As I sit here, writing, overlooking my beautiful farm with my beautiful family, I'm struck with unfathomable gratitude. I'm glad I embarked on that salad dressing journey so long ago. I'm a much different man than I was, and I like this one way better. The struggles always brought me closer to my family. The pain gave me a deeper appreciation for the little things, like the love for your children and the significance of tiny moments of presence. Genevieve always worried that the Tessemae's journey had hardened my heart too much—that I gave too much of myself to the journey. And for a while, she was right, but then the chaos of haters pushed us out, and we found ourselves on a farm. I've never been happier in my life, with wide open spaces and beautiful quiet. Genevieve is a true partner. She never gave up on me and always had faith that I would find my way back to the man she knew I would become. And day by day, I try to add pieces of myself back. I try to live my perfect day every day. I make a conscious effort to soak in every piece of positive energy from my kids. I watch every sunrise and take a walk for every sunset. I advise and help young entrepreneurs to avoid the mistakes I made. I keep everything in perspective and try to not lose sight of the moment. I don't trade time for greed.

Losing a long list of friends helped me to find God and my spirituality, which I never knew I was lacking. I feel completely fulfilled for the first time. My quest to learn the playbook allowed me to write down my own version and teach myself how to fish. My continued quest for knowledge showed me a brave new world of endless possibilities and adventure but with the knowledge of a seasoned guide. I looked back on my life and wouldn't change any of it. My story is not over and continues to unfold daily.

During the dissolve period, I ran into someone who asked me how I was holding up, and I replied, "If I get something from it, great.

If not, it was the longest master's and doctorate program on entrepreneurship in history, and I'm grateful for the lessons learned."

He responded with shock. "Are you kidding me? I'd be fucking dying right now."

Maybe . . . but maybe not.

The End

# Acknowledgments

So many people have come onto the timeline of my life to make this book possible. Here they are, in (approximate) order of appearance in the Tessemae's story.

First and foremost, I want to thank my family. Without us being a unit, we are nothing. Thank you to my parents for being there for us no matter what. We were a lot to handle and you did it with grace. You allowed us to be the men we were destined to be regardless of how hard that was for you both. You were shining examples of what can happen to children when they have amazing parents. Thank you to my brothers Brian and Matthew. I have never met two better men than you both and I never will. Your partnership in this journey we call life has made every step worth it. I am proud to call you my brothers and I am thankful for every day I get to spend with you.

I want to thank my beautiful and magnificent wife Genevieve. God brought you to me and I became complete. Without your love, support, and radiant positivity I would not be the man that I am today. I thank God every day for your love and companionship. And thank you to my beautiful children Broadlee, Severn, Waverley, and Forrest. I live for you. You all showed me what it means to be a man, a leader, a father, and an example. Everything I do is in your honor.

I want to recognize my grandfather, Donald McDonald. You didn't get to see the end of the journey but I couldn't have done it without you. I love and miss you.

A special shout out to the two non-Vetters who have become my family—Kristen Dittami and Moe Taylor. You give me hope in humanity and how wonderful people can be. I am grateful every day you have been in my life.

There are many people who played a positive role in the Tessemae's journey: Jim Chambers, my first investor. You are a true man of honor and you are always right. Brian Toomey, you always believed in me and stepped up when I needed you the most. Justin Smith, if you hadn't taken the dressing this journey never would have started. Bob McDermott, you provided sage advice and counsel during very tough times and I am thankful for your stewardship. Demian Costa, you saw the best in me and stood strong in the storm. You are a wonderful man. Dave Walker, your kindness and positivity will always be appreciated and I am thankful for your support. Hall Chaney, you stepped up when others wouldn't and believed in the journey, and for that I am forever grateful. Krista Mills, you are a ride-or-die chick and I appreciate your dedication to the journey. Channing Cooper, you brought me joy in situations where there wasn't any and I am forever thankful for that. Ken Meyer, you are an amazing friend and supporter of the Vetters. Your dedication to our cause will always be remembered. Tom Bedard, you gave me my first copy of Napoleon Hill's Think and Grow Rich and forever lit a fire in my ass.

Johnson Waite, you were a constant in my life and this journey and I miss you every day. May you rest in peace and watch over us always.

To my YPO forum The Alpha Council, I wouldn't have made it through the storm without you all and I am truly blessed to have you in my life. You enrich my life in ways I didn't think was possible and I am proud to call you my friends.

Dr. Jonathan Fader, this book wouldn't be here without you. I am deeply grateful that you were brought into my life and you make me a better man. Thank you for all you do.

Thank you to my publishing team. At Jenkins Group Book Publishing, Jerry Jenkins and Leah Nicholson, you were an absolute pleasure to work with and your counsel was invaluable. Thanks also my editor, Ellen Neuborne. Who says opposites don't attract? You were the most amazing person to work with and I am deeply grateful you were brought into my life. This book became a book because of your amazing stewardship and ability to appreciate a wild man's story.

To my PR and marketing team, my story can now help others and that is thanks to your abilities. I look forward to many more projects to come.

And last but certainly not least, I want to thank Jesus for coming in to my life when I needed him the most. It was a surprising and unexpected twist of events but made my life deeper, richer, and more meaningful. Happiness and peace are easier with him in my heart.

# About the Author

Gregory Vetter is an innovator and disrupter in the "clean food" movement. His first venture, Tessemae's All Natural broke the rules of the sleepy salad dressing category by using real ingredients and shunning gums and flavor substitutes. He subsequently founded Alta Fresh Food Company, which pioneered a way to get great tasting salads to the masses using an innovative "master kit" process and Home Grown Brand Accelerator, a coaching company empowering the next generation of entrepreneurs. His accolades include Inc Magazine's Entrepreneur of the Year and EY's Entrepreneur of the Year Finalist. He lives in Maryland with his wife and four children.